HOW TO ENJOY YC

VICKY MAUD is Agony Au
many regional newspapers ac
She works extensively on radio and television, using her
counselling training to help listeners and viewers. Vicky is
the UK and European representative on the executive
board of the International Centre for Drug Abuse Preven-
tion in Schools and travels all over the world with this
work. Married with four children, her interests include
travel, reading, tap-dancing, and walking by the sea.

Overcoming Common Problems Series

For a full list of titles please contact
Sheldon Press, Marylebone Road, London NW1 4DU

The Assertiveness Workbook
A plan for busy women
JOANNA GUTMANN

Beating the Comfort Trap
DR WINDY DRYDEN AND JACK
GORDON

Birth Over Thirty Five
SHEILA KITZINGER

Body Language
How to read others' thoughts by their
gestures
ALLAN PEASE

Body Language in Relationships
DAVID COHEN

Calm Down
How to cope with frustration and anger
DR PAUL HAUCK

Cancer – A Family Affair
NEVILLE SHONE

Comfort for Depression
JANET HORWOOD

Coping Successfully with Hayfever
DR ROBERT YOUNGSON

Coping Successfully with Migraine
SUE DYSON

Coping Successfully with Pain
NEVILLE SHONE

Coping Successfully with PMS
KAREN EVENNETT

Coping Successfully with Panic Attacks
SHIRLEY TRICKETT

**Coping Successfully with Prostate
Problems**
ROSY REYNOLDS

**Coping Successfully with Your
Hyperactive Child**
DR PAUL CARSON

**Coping Successfully with Your Irritable
Bowel**
ROSEMARY NICOL

**Coping Successfully with Your Second
Child**
FIONA MARSHALL

Coping with Anxiety and Depression
SHIRLEY TRICKETT

Coping with Blushing
DR ROBERT EDELMANN

Coping with Bronchitis and Emphysema
DR TOM SMITH

Coping with Candida
SHIRLEY TRICKETT

Coping with Chronic Fatigue
TRUDIE CHALDER

Coping with Cot Death
SARAH MURPHY

Coping with Crushes
ANITA NAIK

Coping with Cystitis
CAROLINE CLAYTON

Coping with Depression and Elation
DR PATRICK McKEON

Coping with Postnatal Depression
FIONA MARSHALL

Coping with Psoriasis
PROFESSOR RONALD MARKS

Coping with Schizophrenia
DR STEVEN JONES AND DR FRANK
TALLIS

Coping with Strokes
DR TOM SMITH

Coping with Suicide
DR DONALD SCOTT

Coping with Thyroid Problems
DR JOAN GOMEZ

Coping with Thrush
CAROLINE CLAYTON

Curing Arthritis Exercise Book
MARGARET HILLS AND JANET
HORWOOD

Curing Arthritis Diet Book
MARGARET HILLS

Curing Arthritis – The Drug-Free Way
MARGARET HILLS

Overcoming Common Problems Series

Curing Arthritis
More ways to a drug-free life
MARGARET HILLS

Curing Illness – The Drug-Free Way
MARGARET HILLS

Depression
DR PAUL HAUCK

Divorce and Separation
Every woman's guide to a new life
ANGELA WILLANS

Don't Blame Me!
How to stop blaming yourself and other people
TONY GOUGH

Everything Parents Should Know About Drugs
SARAH LAWSON

Family First Aid and Emergency Handbook
DR ANDREW STANWAY

Getting Along with People
DIANNE DOUBTFIRE

Getting the Best for Your Bad Back
DR ANTHONY CAMPBELL

Good Stress Guide, The
MARY HARTLEY

Heart Attacks – Prevent and Survive
DR TOM SMITH

Helping Children Cope with Bullying
SARAH LAWSON

Helping Children Cope with Divorce
ROSEMARY WELLS

Helping Children Cope with Grief
ROSEMARY WELLS

Hold Your Head Up High
DR PAUL HAUCK

How to Be Your Own Best Friend
DR PAUL HAUCK

How to Cope when the Going Gets Tough
DR WINDY DRYDEN AND JACK GORDON

How to Cope with Bulimia
DR JOAN GOMEZ

How to Cope with Difficult People
ALAN HOUEL WITH CHRISTIAN GODEFROY

How to Cope with Splitting Up
VERA PEIFFER

How to Cope with Stress
DR PETER TYRER

How to Cope with your Child's Allergies
DR PAUL CARSON

How to Do What You Want to Do
DR PAUL HAUCK

How to Improve Your Confidence
DR KENNETH HAMBLY

How to Interview and Be Interviewed
MICHELE BROWN AND GYLES BRANDRETH

How to Keep Your Cholesterol in Check
DR ROBERT POVEY

How to Love and Be Loved
DR PAUL HAUCK

How to Pass Your Driving Test
DONALD RIDLAND

How to Stand up for Yourself
DR PAUL HAUCK

How to Start a Conversation and Make Friends
DON GABOR

How to Stop Smoking
GEORGE TARGET

How to Stop Worrying
DR FRANK TALLIS

How to Survive Your Teenagers
SHEILA DAINOW

How to Untangle Your Emotional Knots
DR WINDY DRYDEN AND JACK GORDON

How to Write a Successful CV
JOANNA GUTMANN

Hysterectomy
SUZIE HAYMAN

Is HRT Right for You?
DR ANNE MACGREGOR

The Incredible Sulk
DR WINDY DRYDEN

The Irritable Bowel Diet Book
ROSEMARY NICOL

The Irritable Bowel Stress Book
ROSEMARY NICOL

Overcoming Common Problems Series

Overcoming Common Problems

HOW TO ENJOY
YOUR RETIREMENT

Vicky Maud

First published in Great Britain 1996
Sheldon Press, SPCK, Marylebone Road, London NW1 4DU

British Library Cataloguing-in-Publication Data
A catalogue record for this book is available from the British Library
ISBN 0–85969–740–1

Photoset by Deltatype Ltd, Ellesmere Port, Cheshire
Printed in Great Britain by Biddles Ltd, Guildford and King's Lynn

*with love to my husband Ken, who is always
there for me, and my children
Philip, Louise, John and Lucy,
who I am very proud of.*

Acknowledgements

When I first sat down to write this book I thought it would be hard but it turned into a very enjoyable task.

My thanks go to Sue Dobson, Editor of *Choice* Magazine, who inspired readers to write in with their experiences. As ever, *Choice* readers responded warmly and swiftly, and without their stories this book would not be complete.

Acknowledgments go to Pharmacia & Upjohn, LRC Products and Masters & Johnson for their help with information.

My grateful thanks to Linda who typed my manuscript so superbly whilst listening to my muffled voice on tape, and to Jeananne who stopped me from losing it on several occasions!

A big thank you to Ann Lovell who was always at the end of the phone when I needed support.

Finally but by no means least, thanks to my husband, Ken, who looked after the children and cooked meals on countless occasions so that I could write this book, and for his constant love and encouragement.

Contents

Introduction

Dear Friend

My name is Vicky Maud and for the past 15 years I have been working as an Agony Aunt in magazines, newspapers and on radio and television.

My work as a counsellor and as Agony Aunt on *Choice* magazine has brought me in contact with many people who are about to retire, or who already have. It has become increasingly apparent that although many people get the practical things sorted out when they retire, very few look at the emotional side. So this book is entirely about the feelings that surround retirement. Each chapter will help you to explore your feelings and will end with a selection of problem letters I have received which are relevant to that chapter, and my answers, which I hope may be of help.

This book is about new beginnings and the adventurous road ahead. It is about casting away constraints and embarking on a road of discovery. It is not about accepting a back seat in life because you no longer work, and not about being thought of as old or past it. Certainly not about feeling like a second-class citizen or being too old for a loving or sexual relationship. Even if this is the way you feel at the moment, I hope through this book I will help you to think differently and positively.

If you have ever stood on a hill and watched the dawn break on a new day and felt a feeling of excitement rising in you, then this is definitely the book for you as you stand on the threshold of retirement. Some of you will have longed for retirement, others will have been dreading it, but you all have in common the journey that you are setting out on.

How you use that journey is up to you, but it is normal, even if the prospect of retirement excites you, to feel a bit apprehensive as well. Ahead of you everything may be unknown, but how exciting to be starting a new part of your life with all the challenges it will bring. Challenges that will help to keep you active, healthy, alert, happy and fulfilled.

This book is not about finances, pensions, benefits or investments, although we may touch on them as we go along. Those subjects have already been well covered in other books. This book is about people like you, your choices and having the right attitude towards life and the retirement years, whatever your situation, so that you can get the most from them. These are your years – they belong to you! Maybe for the first time in your life you will be able to put yourself first.

This book is about feelings and emotions. Some that you may never have experienced before; some you may feel guilty about. It is also about feeling good about yourself and your retirement so that you live life to the full rather than just exist. The very fact that you have this book in your hands shows that you want to enjoy the years ahead and are prepared to adjust both emotionally and practically to get this.

So, as you embark on this journey into retirement, maybe with some worries, let us just look at all that has gone beforehand and build on the resources of your lifetime.

Cast your mind back if you can to the day that you started school with an unknown path ahead. You probably felt frightened, even if you put a brave face on it for your mum. Up until then you had been with her for most of the time. Then suddenly you were dumped with 30 other nervous children and an adult that you had never met before who not only expected you to do everything he or she told you to but also to be good into the bargain, a tall order at five years of age. But you coped, made friends, passed exams and even managed to enjoy yourself for some of the time.

Somewhere between the ages of 15 and 18 you were faced with another crisis: having got used to school life, you expected to walk bravely into the 'workplace' or 'college'. From being one of the school community to being 'on your own' was yet another step into the unknown which you accepted with a challenge.

Whether you chose marriage or live-in relationships over the years, it took some getting used to, being one of a couple. It was something you went into with love in your heart and maybe stars in your eyes. Romance is made of wonderful stuff, but the day-to-day road of living together did take a lot of effort to make it work.

More avenues opened up ahead when you found you were to be a parent. Yet what exciting ones! The joy of seeing your baby for the first time, the fears when you felt things were not going right, the proud feelings as you watched your children grow, knowing you had given them life and done your best from those first floundering moments you held them to the times when they came to you for advice.

Many of you will have had devastating events in your lives. Maybe divorce, separation, illness or the loss of a child or your partner. No previous experience could have prepared you for this. Once again you were thrown into a situation you found hard to cope with, but cope you did and learnt a lot in the process.

Throughout your lives many of you would have worked full or part time, you may have moaned from time to time; you may have felt hard done by, especially if money was short and no one seemed to understand how difficult things were for you.

So many demands on your time and energy over the years and very little time for yourself and the things that you wanted to do. Throughout your life you have faced many challenges and changes of direction – retirement is just another!

You may feel nervous . . . but you were on the day you started school! You may feel as if you are stepping into the unknown . . . but isn't that how you felt on your first day of work? Deep down you may feel excited . . . remember when you first fell in love . . . and your wedding day!

How will I feel in all those empty hours and days ahead? Remember how you longed for some time to yourself when the children were so demanding or the boss gave you a hard time? Now you can have it!

You may feel that all the good times have come to an end with the loss of status and companionship at work, but be honest with yourself, haven't you felt like this at other times in your life and then gone on to find something even better?

Life is a journey paved with interesting destinations. Retirement is part of this. Before you lies a long, clear sandy path on which you will leave your footprints. The dawn is breaking on a new beginning in your life. This time you are armed with the experiences of a lifetime. Take a step forward and recognize these feelings as excitement rather than worries. The path ahead is firm and sunny and through this book I will help you to make your retirement definitely the best years of your life!

Kind regards

Vicky

1

Are you ready to retire?

Joe pedalled off to work, sandwiches in rucksack slung over his back, just as he had done every day for the past 49 years. Today was much the same as any other Friday, the traffic was heavy, tempers were frayed and it threatened to rain before he got to the factory. Not far behind in her car was his wife Mary on her way to the secondary school where she taught French. Looking at either of them, no one would pick them out as being any different from any of the other commuters, but for Joe and Mary this was their last day at work before retiring. They both felt a mixture of excitement, happiness, relief, apprehension, sadness and anxiety, all normal feelings and very common when people are about to retire. Very few people can give up on their working life without experiencing some of these emotions, if not all of them. How you approach and deal with retirement will depend on several factors:

- how much your job and the status it brings matter to you;
- whether you will miss the structure of your day and the colleagues you are leaving behind;
- whether you love or hate your job.

You may feel ready for a rest or a change of direction, or, on the other hand, you may well be dreading it. The fact that you will be spending more time at home means a good relationship with your partner is very important. By good I don't mean perfect. The relationship has to be an honest, open and loving one that can withstand any compromises and hurdles it may have to face. The way you feel both at work and in your relationship will determine how you are going to cope initially when you retire. You have to be totally honest to be able to set out on the adventurous road ahead; it doesn't matter if you come across obstacles, at least you will be recognizing them and in doing so you will find a way to overcome them. Everyone needs encouragement to step into the unknown and this is what I hope to help you to do with confidence. Don't push little doubts away, they need to be faced up to and dealt with.

How do you feel about retirement?

If I was to ask you how you felt about your retirement the chances are I would get one of two responses: either 'Fine, fine' or 'I am not sure'; a few of you might say 'Can't wait' or 'I'm dreading it'. To help you find out where you are emotionally in your life at the moment, I would like you to answer honestly the following questions. Go with your gut feeling, don't stop and think about the answers, tick spontaneously one box for each question. Although these questions are aimed mainly at men and women who are about to retire, those already retired may like to do them as well to see if they feel any different now to the day when they retired. At the end you will see how to add up your score and what your score means.

Q.1 Do you wish your life had been different?

(a) Yes, I would change most things.
(b) I am not one to dwell on the past.
(c) No, I'm totally satisfied with my life.

Q.2 Do you have friends?

(a) No, I don't need friends.
(b) I wish I had more.
(c) Yes, lots.

Q.3 How do you see the future?

(a) I am dreading it.
(b) I try to be positive.
(c) Everything will be great.

Q.4 Are you looking forward to retirement?

(a) I am not sure.
(b) No.
(c) Yes.

Q.5 How prepared are you for retirement?

(a) I try not to think about it.
(b) I worry about it.
(c) I have been on a pre-retirement course.

Q.6 Do you look forward to going to work each day?

(a) Never.
(b) Sometimes.
(c) Yes.

Q.7 How important is your status at work?

(a) I have no status.
(b) Unimportant.
(c) Very important.

Q.8 Will you miss your colleagues?

(a) Not sure.
(b) No.
(c) Yes.

Q.9 Do you have any hobbies?

(a) None.
(b) Trying to find some.
(c) Lots.

Q.10 What bothers you most?

(a) My age.
(b) My fitness.
(c) My looks.

Q.11 Are you prone to mood swings and depression?

(a) Seldom.
(b) Sometimes.
(c) Never.

Q.12 How often do you laugh?

(a) Never.
(b) Occasionally.
(c) Frequently.

Q.13 Are you happy with your relationship?

(a) No.
(b) It could be better.
(c) Yes.

Q.14 How do you and your partner get on?

(a) Not very well.
(b) Reasonably well.
(c) Very well.

Q.15 Does your partner irritate you?

(a) Yes, always.
(b) Yes, sometimes.
(c) No, never.

Q.16 Do you feel angry with your partner?

(a) Often.
(b) Sometimes.
(c) Never.

Q.17 Do you show your anger?

(a) No.
(b) Sometimes.
(c) Often.

Q.18 Can you talk to your partner about your feelings?

(a) I don't want to, they wouldn't understand.
(b) Yes.
(c) No, I wouldn't want to worry them.

Q.19 Do you listen to your partner?

(a) No, I can't be bothered.
(b) I try.
(c) Yes, I always listen.

Q.20 Do you enjoy sex?

(a) Not interested.
(b) Tolerate it.
(c) Enjoy it.

Q.21 Does your partner enjoy sex?

(a) Not interested.
(b) Tolerates it.
(c) Enjoys it.

Q.22 Do you love your partner?

(a) No.
(b) Not sure.
(c) Yes.

Q.23 Do you feel taken for granted?

(a) Always.
(b) Sometimes.
(c) Never.

Q.24 Is your partner romantic?

(a) No, never.
(b) Only occasionally.
(c) Yes, often.

Q.25 Which is most important to you?

(a) Friends.
(b) Family.
(c) Your partner.

Q.26 Do you worry about getting old?

(a) Often.
(b) Sometimes.
(c) Never.

Now that you have ticked one answer in each section, go through and add up your score. You should give yourself:

1 point for every (a) ticked
2 points for every (b) ticked
3 points for every (c) ticked

Now add up your total points.

If you scored between 61 and 78

With a score like this you bring a lot of confidence to your retirement, but don't be too complacent; you may feel you have got everything under control but sometimes even the best-laid plans can go awry. You need to be very aware of your partner's feelings because they may not have the same positive attitude as you do. Look after your health by learning to relax, otherwise you may find even small setbacks make you very stressed. You have the inner strength that is needed for a good happy retirement providing you use it wisely, but you may need to make some emotional adjustments along the way. If you scored 75 or over you need to hang on to that 'cloud nine' in case you get knocked off!

If you scored between 40 and 60

You fall into the most realistic category of people because you recognize your strengths and weaknesses. However, you can be indecisive so it is important to become more of a 'planner' and less of a 'wait-and-see person'. You tend to hold yourself back rather than pushing yourself forward, so remember to try and boost your own confidence. Showing your feelings more often may surprise or shock your partner but it may also clear away some of the cobwebs that have collected over the years. You will be happy in retirement so long as your relationship is good; don't put up with second best which is an easy option. Always try to make the most of each day and talk to your partner about things that please you or make you unhappy. You certainly need a lot of love and kindness in your life.

If you scored 39 or under

It is all out there waiting for you if only you can get your act together and stop thinking that the best in life is for other people. Retirement for you will bring many new beginnings but first you have to sort out your emotions and maybe your relationship with your partner. You can be a willing victim at times and you do need to stand up for yourself more often. There is no such thing as 'too late' when it comes to retirement; this is a new start which will give you a second chance to do the things you have always wanted to do. Take a more active role in your relationship rather than just letting things happen around you. The future has much to offer if you make some effort yourself now.

Making the transition

The transition from working life to being retired can be a difficult time: one day you are part of a working team, next day a gold watch and a sendoff, later you are at home with all the excitement behind you.

Let's look at the sendoff first. Most companies plan a small party of some kind to say farewell to the person who is retiring. The problem is this is often not what the retiring person wants. Many people say they would rather disappear quietly and perhaps have a get-together a few weeks after their retirement. If you feel like this, then you should say how you feel, but remember the sendoff is as much for your friends and colleagues as it is for you. They want the opportunity to say goodbye and how much they have enjoyed working with you. If the speech is bothering you, then just keep it short and simple and don't feel you have to reminisce or entertain the audience.

How you will react when the time comes to leave will depend very much on whether you enjoy your job and status. If you have been in a position of authority with people looking to you for answers and with respect, then you will miss this even if it seemed a bit of a drag at the time. Powerful positions do a lot to boost the ego and when this is taken away you can feel very flat inside. This won't happen immediately. For a while you may talk about your work and the responsibility you held to those you meet, but as it dwindles into the past you will find it leaves a gap. Most people like to feel special in some way or another and up until now your job has provided this. Gradually you will adjust, but own up to any feelings of loss – don't pretend they're not there. Say 'I miss my job' if this is the case, then find other ways of fulfilling your needs. I wonder how many times you have turned the alarm clock off in the morning only to wish you could go back to sleep and didn't have to go to work. Your days may have been packed and interesting, or they may have seemed long and rather dull. It depends on how they were as to whether you will be glad to be free of them or not. You may miss the high-pressured meetings with the long business lunches on expense accounts, days entertaining clients, playing golf or business trips abroad, but if you have been stuck on an assembly line for 30-odd years doing a repetitive job you may feel a tremendous relief at being free. Likewise a teacher may miss the children she taught but a retiring doctor may be glad not to have to turn out at all times of the day and night.

If you haven't retired yet, now is the time to start planning. Not only for the practicalities, but also for your emotional needs. Pre-retirement classes are available through companies, Continuing Education Centres and through the Pre-Retirement Association. You could also ask your employer if they offer pre-retirement courses for staff. Some people decide to work a shorter week for a few weeks before they retire to break themselves in gently. If this appeals to you, ask your employer if you can work for three or four days a week towards the end of your employment. Obviously finances need to be taken into account, and don't do anything that could affect your pension rights. Some people retire and their employers continue to employ them on a contract or part-time basis. This can also help the emotional adjustment that is needed.

What you don't want to feel when you retire is lost or useless, so you need to get the right attitude before you leave. To help you do this I want you to keep a diary over the last few weeks or months that you work. This is your 'mind exploration diary' and a very important one. Note down each day how you feel emotionally after what has happened during the day. Maybe it has been a good day and you felt great or something could have gone wrong which made you feel fed up. Once you have written down your thoughts, draw a line under them and write how you would have liked to have spent the day if you hadn't had to go to work. Be honest, put exactly what you feel even though it may seem far-fetched, fantasy or out of character.

The idea of this exercise is to allow your mind to explore your innermost thoughts and dreams without feeling guilty or repressed. Although you will know that some of your dreams will never become a reality, it will stimulate you into thinking about the things that might be possible. At the same time it will help you to focus on what you are leaving behind and help you to let go more easily. Too many people push retirement into the back of their mind and when the day finally arrives they fall into retirement rather like an egg being pushed from a nest by a cuckoo. Then they feel lost because they no longer have the structure and stimulus of a working life. Those who have planned and given it a lot of thought will most likely be the ones who are looking forward to retiring. Hopefully, they will have taken up interests and made plans that will help them to step into retirement with confidence.

Postbag

Q.1 I have told my wife that I am looking forward to retiring, but to be honest I am in a real state over it. I met a friend who retired eight months ago and he says there is no point to his life any more, he says the highlight of his week is when he buys his lottery ticket.

It is a pity you bumped into this 'prophet of doom' . . . poor man! Life sounds pretty miserable for him but that need not apply to you, life is what you make it. If you are positive and determined to have a purpose to your life, it can be even more fulfilling than when you worked. Instead of letting him get you down, use him as a role model of how you are not going to be!

Q.2 My family have always been supportive of my work, and my wife and I have a very close loving relationship. I once heard my wife telling a girlfriend that she was 'turned on' by the fact that I was so high powered in my job. At the time, this pleased me but now I worry she might go off me once I retire and I don't do my job.

The person to be telling this to is your wife. You overheard 'girls' talk' and you were flattered by it. If you hadn't, then you would have been none the wiser and would have accepted your relationship for what it is – a good one. Tell her how you feel, she won't stop loving you.

Q.3 There is a chap in my office who is to take over my job when I retire. I can't stand him and never have. He puts as little effort into his work as he can yet he is the first to run others down, it really bugs me that he is being given my patch which I have built up from nothing. Any one else I could have shown the ropes willingly, but not this one. How can I get over these angry, even violent feelings, towards him? The boss thinks he is wonderful.

I think there is more to this than you admit. Maybe you feel you have been cheated or unjustly treated in the past, or that everything falls into his lap while you have had to put in a lot of effort. You can't change him or the way the boss treats him. These feelings will eat away at you if you let them. Don't spoil your good record now, rise above it, show him around your patch and be proud of it, then walk away knowing you always gave of your best.

Q.4 I have been going out with a man at the office for the past three months. We are both divorced, we get on well and as we are both due to retire soon he has suggested we sell our homes and move into a house together. Do you think this a good idea?
You don't mention love or any romantic attachments. Take this one step at a time, give the relationship a few more months before deciding anything, certainly until you have both been retired for a while. Don't rush into anything.

Retirement is one of the most important parts of your life. People are living longer, staying healthier and expecting a good quality of life; no one should see this period of their life as one to dread or the beginning of the end – that is the wrong attitude. Look at your questionnaire from time to time to see if your attitudes change as you reach retirement, and keep your exploration diary at hand and note down any thoughts that please or worry you. This way you are acknowledging your thoughts rather than letting them slip back unnoticed and undealt with in your subconscious. Involve your partner in your plans, if something is worrying you talk it through together so that you can both be happy when your retirement day arrives.

2
How are your relationships?

It may be rather early in this book to ask you to jump into the deep end of the pool of truth to look at your marriage or relationship . . . but that is exactly what I want you to do!

If you can't face doing this, then test the water first and let yourself gradually enter what, for you, might be the first truthful look at your relationship in a long, long while.

When you have been married for a long time, are in a second marriage, or are in a live-in relationship, retirement is going to affect you both even though one of you may be continuing to work. I have lost count of the number of letters I have received from men and women alike who have found retirement puts great strain on the relationship, and even more who have chosen to ignore the problems over the years only to find these magnify once the couple retire and are together for most of the time.

It would be easy for me to say make time for each other and have time for yourself and everything will be all right, but that would be ducking the issue and that is not what you have spent good money on this book for. So let's get on with it and look at your relationship.

During the next few weeks I want you to make a plan of your life and how it has been over the years. To do this you will need a sheet of A4 paper. Lay it horizontally on a table, draw a horizontal line across the centre of the paper and write 'Happy times' above the line and 'Sad times' below the line on the far left-hand side so that it looks like Table 1.

The line along the centre represents you and your feelings on an even path. Things that happen in our life and our relationships can make us feel happy or sad to a greater or lesser degree, so feelings can range above the line from happy to ecstatic and below the line from sad to depressed or suicidal. What you have to do is to plot the events, feelings, achievements, disappointments, relationships, affairs, compensations, bereavements, happy events, satisfactions and any other feelings on this chart.

A chart like this is a personal thing and it will enable you to be honest with yourself without feeling threatened. No one else need see it. Do it when you are alone and have plenty of time. This chart will only open up a small part of you, later you will find you will

Happy times

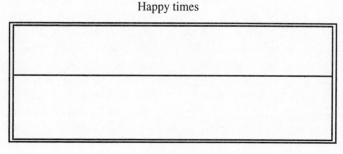

Sad times

Table 1 Sample life plan

remember far more things and feel safe to plot them on your chart. So you will need to start again with several pieces of A4 paper sellotaped together or perhaps a long sheet of lining or wallpaper.

For now, start with the A4 page. To begin with, put a dot on the page near the beginning of the line on the far left-hand side, put a note when you met your partner. Depending on the circumstances, your dot will either be on the line or above or below it, depending on how you felt at the time. Now move on to how you felt when you married, and through your feelings, up until the present time.

Tables 2, 3 and 4 are some examples of other people's charts which may help you to understand the process and what to do.

A relationship chart like this will help you to be honest with yourself without it feeling threatening. How often have you managed to do this before? It will also guide you through your emotions so that you can better understand what makes your life unbearable, sad or happy. Most of us cruise through life and what hurts us we put to the backs of our mind. This way we don't have to make decisions or do anything about the problems. We mould our lives in such a way that we can cope and things are familiar to us, but when our lives radically change such as with retirement, it can cause havoc not only with our day-to-day life but particularly with our emotions. If you don't recognize and deal with the problem areas of your life and your emotions, then the chances are the problems will increase when you and your partner are together 24 hours a day.

Kevin

Let's look at Kevin's case first (see Table 2). All his life Kevin let things happen around him. He never took charge of his life. He drifted into a relationship with Elaine as if it was out of his control. Even though he had doubts about marrying Elaine in the first instance, he let himself be swept into the marriage. After six years he was unhappy, dissatisfied and he just accepted this as his lot in life. Even through constant rows and depression he still let everything happen around him. Even the affair he got into was instigated by the woman; when he realized he loved her he still couldn't make a decision to leave a loveless marriage. Years later, on the brink of retirement, he had so many regrets and feared he had left it too late to change his life. The truth is, he hadn't.

It is never too late to make changes. It was pretty obvious that neither Kevin nor Elaine were happy. There was no love, no sex, just tolerance of the relationship. If they were to stay together and have at the very least a reasonable relationship they needed to talk about the past, what they felt was wrong with the relationship and how they could make a future together. Kevin needed to start to make decisions even if small ones. He had to decide how his time would be spent, whether he could be with Elaine all or part of the time. She had to do the same and both had to do it with respect and consideration for each other without letting hurt feelings overshadow the whole purpose of the discussion.

Kevin and Elaine did this with the help of a Relate counsellor and they are now three years into retirement together. They also sought help from a sex therapist and things have improved. Elaine had lost respect for Kevin over the years, she felt he was weak, and although she knew she bossed and pushed him around, she hated him for letting her do it. Although hurt and angry when he admitted having had an affair it made her look at him with new eyes, she hadn't expected this of him, but she wasn't surprised that even then he couldn't make a decision, it had to be made for him by the other woman when she walked away. Kevin has made great strides towards becoming more decisive. In fact, it has become a bit of a family joke. They both feel they drifted into their relationship which has been a disappointment for both of them. Having admitted this to each other they then decided to give the relationship another try hoping that this new-found honesty would help.

16

KEVIN

Married 26 years. 2 children. 2 grandchildren. Bank Manager

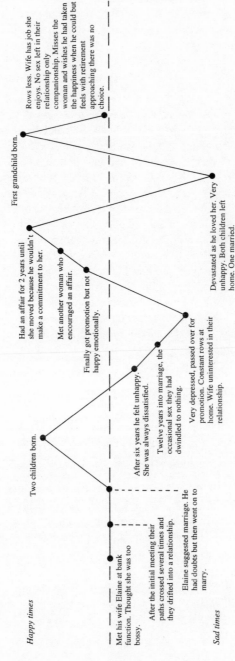

Happy times

Met his wife Elaine at bank function. Thought she was too bossy.

After the initial meeting their paths crossed several times and they drifted into a relationship.

Elaine suggested marriage. He had doubts but then went on to marry.

Sad times

Two children born.

After six years he felt unhappy. She was always dissatisfied.

Twelve years into marriage, the occasional sex they had dwindled to nothing.

Very depressed, passed over for promotion. Constant rows at home. Wife uninterested in their relationship.

Finally got promotion but not happy emotionally.

Met another woman who encouraged an affair.

Had an affair for 2 years until she moved because he wouldn't make a commitment to her.

First grandchild born.

Devastated as he loved her. Very unhappy. Both children left home. One married.

Rows less. Wife has job she enjoys. No sex left in their relationship only companionship. Misses the woman and wishes he had taken the happiness when he could but feels with retirement approaching there was no choice.

Table 2 Kevin's life plan

17

Within every relationship there are dynamics between the couple that are responsible for the way the relationship goes. The balance of these has changed in Elaine and Kevin's relationship and they are much happier together.

John

John's story (see Table 3) is littered with sadness, disappointment and guilt: guilt over his girlfriend's death, guilt and disappointment at not being able to father Sally's children, sadness at Sally's illness, guilt that he isn't there to care for her and guilt that he is not telling his present wife Joan when he keeps in touch with Sally. This is their situation at the time of writing this book. What could be a good relationship to enter retirement with is being spoilt by these guilty feelings and Joan's insecurity over his ex-wife. John needs to allow himself to dump these guilty feelings; fate took his girlfriend away from him all those years ago but it let John keep his life. Guilty and sad feelings are keeping him locked into a spiral of depression and low self-esteem. Replacing these by remembering the good times they had together not only lifts the depression but is a fine tribute to her life. Being unable to father children was a disappointment, but he should think about the good it brought. John and Sally would never have adopted Jason and given him a loving family life if there had been children of their own.

Redundancy has brought misery to many people, it has struck rich and poor homes and men and women of all ages and status. The key factor in many redundancies is to save money, there is nothing personal in the majority of redundancies. In fact most people will say redundancies are jolly impersonal when they are carried out. Because Sally and John parted as friends the link of the years they spent together is still there. Joan's insecurity is understandable, friendship means caring, caring implies closeness, closeness could lead to intimacy. All reassurance must come from John, not only in words but in actions as well. He must recognize Joan's fears and put her feelings first, as she is his wife now. To ask John to turn his back on his sick ex-wife would be useless. Sally needs to be assured that support will be there for her, but from then on it should be as a couple if Joan will agree to this. If she agrees, Sally will cease to be a rival and Joan will feel more in control of her feelings and of their situation.

JOHN

Married twice. Divorced after 15 years. Married second time for 7 years. One adopted child. Works in car showroom.

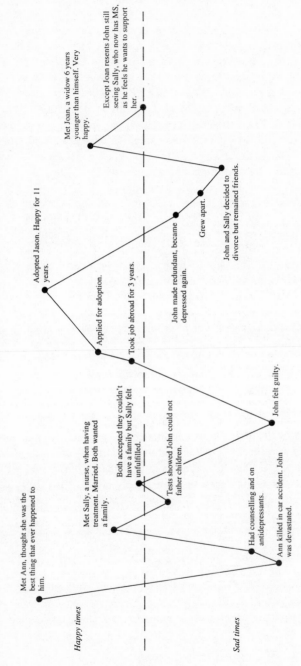

Happy times

Sad times

Met Ann, thought she was the best thing that ever happened to him.

Met Sally, a nurse, when having treatment. Married. Both wanted a family.

Both accepted they couldn't have a family but Sally felt unfulfilled.

Applied for adoption.

Adopted Jason. Happy for 11 years.

Took job abroad for 3 years.

John made redundant, became depressed again.

Grew apart.

John and Sally decided to divorce but remained friends.

Met Joan, a widow 6 years younger than himself. Very happy.

Except Joan resents John still seeing Sally, who now has MS, as he feels he wants to support her.

Tests showed John could not father children.

Ann killed in car accident. John was devastated.

Had counselling and on antidepressants.

John felt guilty.

Table 3 John's life plan

19

Mary

Reading through Mary's case history gave me a feeling of someone who had resigned herself to being told what to do all the time and accepting decisions being made for her, even though she disagreed with them (see Table 4). Paul is a man who likes to be in charge and feel that he knows what is best for the family. Because Mary never challenged him, or any of the decisions he made, he just assumed that she was in agreement. Mary is a willing victim to a certain degree of dominance within the relationship. Paul makes no effort to show his feelings because Mary doesn't give out the vibes that she needs love and emotional stimulation, and never has.

Why didn't she stick out for a church wedding? Why did she agree to marry him if he wasn't the romantic type of man that she needed? Why had she never asked him about his feelings for her? Why did she let him decide whether she should have a job or not? Probably because she felt his strength of character overwhelmed hers and so she accepted rather than having her say.

Mary needs to sort this out before Paul retires otherwise she is going to be trapped even more in a confining relationship. Maybe if she said no just once in her life she would shake things up, toss their relationship into the air so that when it came down again the power within the relationship would be more evenly distributed. Paul has been the provider and the protector for many years; he has also worked in a job which has brought him into contact with the bad things in life as well as given him control over people in different situations. Sometimes working in professions like his spills over into family life. Paul may have found it hard to switch his manner at home and may have felt that he had to protect Mary and the children from the dangers that he met every day. Hence he makes all the decisions. Perhaps if Mary says no occasionally or gets a part-time job, it will alter the relationship. Paul won't want things to change, but in the long run the relationship will be healthier and it will stand more of a chance in retirement. At the same time, Paul will need reassurance that Mary still needs him. Paul may start to admire his wife rather than take her for granted. It may even help him to see that she is a person in her own right, that he can respect her and hopefully tell her the three words that she has been waiting to hear – I love you.

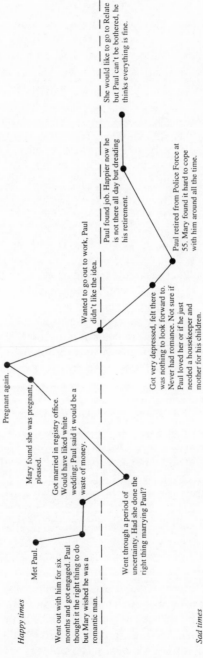

MARY

Married. Drifted into marrying Paul.

Happy times

Met Paul.

Went out with him for six months and got engaged. Paul thought it the right thing to do but Mary wished he was a romantic man.

Mary found she was pregnant, pleased.

Got married in registry office. Would have liked white wedding; Paul said it would be a waste of money.

Pregnant again.

Went through a period of uncertainty. Had she done the right thing marrying Paul?

Wanted to go out to work, Paul didn't like the idea.

Got very depressed, felt there was nothing to look forward to. Never had romance. Not sure if Paul loved her or if he just needed a housekeeper and mother for his children.

Paul found job. Happier now he is not there all day but dreading his retirement.

Paul retired from Police Force at 55. Mary found it hard to cope with him around all the time.

She would like to go to Relate but Paul can't be bothered, he thinks everything is fine.

Sad times

Table 4 Mary's life plan

21

Unhappy feelings

When you make your chart you will be surprised how much the feelings that surround each event in your life will flood back. You may have kept these feelings hidden for years. If they hurt or make you feel uncomfortable leave them alone for a day or so and then go back. Gradually you will cope with them and in doing so you will gather strength.

Once you have identified the things that are spoiling your relationship and making you unhappy, it is up to you to look at ways of working on these to get the balance right. Don't expect miracles! I have yet to meet anyone who has a 100 per cent perfect relationship. Talking to your partner about feelings may not be easy. They may say it comes as a shock to them that you are unhappy, but if they are really honest with themselves, deep down they knew. They may, like you, have been pushing their regrets, indecisions, disappointments and anger into the depths of their subconscious, a bit like a rubbish tip for feelings they couldn't deal with.

If you find that your partner is having an affair, or has had one, the emotions that you feel will be similar to most of the other problems we have looked at so far. There will be grief as in bereavement, but for the loss of what you had and what might have been. You will feel rejection, and loneliness will set in the moment you find out. No one can tell you what to do, it is something you have to work out for yourself. Although most people lay the blame for the affair firmly at the door of one partner, in most cases the reasons for an affair are joint ones arising from problems within the marriage or relationship. Whether it is lack of sex, interest or caring, or is about being taken for granted, or boredom, this has to be seen as a joint problem if there is to be any chance of the marriage being able to change, for change is what is needed.

Secondly, it is important to think before you say or do anything. Ask yourself if your marriage is worth fighting for. If it is, then that is what you have to do; seek counselling, be willing to talk and to listen. Say how you feel and ask questions that you feel will help solve the problem, not ones that are just going to turn the knife and make your pain worse. For instance, many men and women have affairs after retirement because they feel the need to prove to themselves that they are still attractive and desirable. Asking if they felt taken for granted, unloved or not desirable will bring forth far more positive responses than asking if sex was better with the other person than it was with you. In their fifties, sixties or seventies they may still need to prove something to themselves.

Very few people leave their partners to be with their lovers or mistresses after an affair. Although an attraction is obviously there, and

22

they still want some love and excitement, in most cases they value their roots in their marriage and are reluctant to leave. If they can rekindle love and excitement in their marriage, most men and women will choose to stay if their partner still wants them. Counselling with Relate ranks the best for help with marital problems and especially with affairs. Sometimes it will lead to a divorce, but even then Relate can help couples to separate or divorce amicably. Like a bereavement, a divorce takes you through a whole range of emotions, including shock, disbelief that it is happening, loss of confidence, rejection, depression, anger, anxiety and fear. Add to this the loss of status, possible loss of home, money problems and having to learn to be single again, is it any wonder that many divorcees become nervous, tense, agitated, lonely, depressed and unconfident. Having been one of a couple it is amazing how people's attitudes change towards you once you are on your own. Friends may be worried that you could be after their partner or that divorce is some sort of disease that they could catch, whilst others take it upon themselves to sit in judgement and tell you where you went wrong.

I had a very sad letter from a woman called Nancy who was 68 and whose 66-year-old husband had divorced her for another woman. Totally shattered by what had happened, she went to stay with a friend who told her 'no man goes for another woman unless you've let yourself go, you look frumpy or you've lost interest in sex'. Already teetering on the brink of despair, this totally destroyed any self-confidence Nancy had left.

If you are faced with the possibility of divorce, for whatever reason, do stop and look at ways of repairing the relationship before totally giving up on it. Ask yourself if the reasons for divorce outweigh those for staying together. Are you are prepared to fight for your marriage? What changes are you prepared to make to repair it? It is no good digging in your heels and dumping all the blame on to your partner or having a 'holier than thou' attitude but offering to forgive if they stay and abide by the rules. I have lost count of the number of letters I have received from people saying they are willing to forgive providing, . . .! This throws up barriers against reconciliation before you even start; better to say 'Let's look at where we are, why we are there, what we can do about it and what we want to do about it'. With age should come wisdom and understanding and the ability to talk things through. If you find yourself heading for the divorce courts, take time to look at your relationship to see if it is scratched or totally broken. No one needs to stay in an unhappy marriage, but be sure the unhappiness is not of your own making.

When there is mental or physical violence and abuse I don't think you have to put up with this. Many have stayed because of the children, hoping the violence would go, but it doesn't.

Sheila was 64 when she decided to leave Tom. The dentist told her he couldn't save her front teeth following a beating from Tom and she decided that enough was enough. She left to live temporarily with her daughter, and divorced him. She told me she finally plucked up courage to go but it took two broken arms, dozens of black eyes, cuts and bruises, loose teeth and a perforated ear drum before she could do it. Tom said she angered him because she was so timid, now he says he respects her for standing up to him. Sheila says it is too late and she has got a job in a launderette to supplement her pension.

Before retirement, it is an easy option to chug along with things as they are. Retirement is going to change things completely, it could last for a third of your life!

Postbag

Q.1 I am due to retire in six months. My wife has made it obvious that she intends to do her 'own thing', as she puts it, when I retire. She says having me around all the time will put a strain on her nerves. We have grown apart over the years, I don't know why we are still together. There is no love or affection. I bring the money home, she cooks and looks after the house. She goes out with her girlfriends from work once a week and to see our daughter on Saturdays. I go to football occasionally but that is all. Retirement seems a pretty bleak prospect.

From what you say, I can understand why. You have three choices. Yes, you can stay together and put up with things as they are, you can separate, or you can make changes. How? By talking to your wife and together working out when things started to go wrong and why. Maybe she feels taken for granted, unloved and neglected, perhaps you feel she only wants you for the money, that she has no respect for you, or that she excludes you from her life. It is a bit like an illness. Ignore the symptoms and it gets worse. Bring them out into the open and you can find the treatment. The same goes for relationships. You will be surprised at the number of couples who do not realize that they are both unhappy because of misunderstandings or inconsiderate behaviour. With honesty and a bit more give and take, the relationship can alter.

Q.2 I know I have been unfair to my wife over the years, I have had affairs and kept her short of money when the children were small. She never complained and I despised her for letting me walk all over her. Because of this I treated her with contempt. When she became ill a year ago I was frightened I was going to lose her, I wanted to make everything up to her, I bought her flowers and presents, I was nice to her. This confused her and she told our daughter that she must be dying for me to act in this way and she was scared, so I reverted to form. She, thank God, got better. We are both retired and have been for years. I want to make up for the past, but now I don't know how to do it.

To change that much overnight would be a shock for anyone. You have to do it slowly but surely. Try to find small ways of pleasing her and bringing happiness into her life. Maybe a cup of tea when she looks tired, the offer to take her out for a meal or for the day occasionally. Try to say at least one nice thing to her each day and remember to say thank you for what she does for you. If you can gain her confidence slowly, then things will snowball from there. One day you may feel that you want to say sorry, but actions often say more than words.

Q.3 When I divorced my husband 15 years ago I got custody of our 11-year-old daughter. I took her to the United States where I met and married my late husband. On our return to the UK my daughter wanted to contact her father but I told her I had no idea where he was and she accepted this. A year later, she told me she had traced her dad, had met him and that he wanted to see me. It took a lot of persuasion on her part but in the end I agreed. Since then we have done things together as a family, even though we live apart; birthdays, holidays, outings are shared and he and I meet for dinner every Saturday evening. On several occasions we have slept together, we get on better than we ever did. He has now asked me to marry him but I am scared that things might go back to being as awful as they used to be. Yet if he disappears from my life I know I would be devastated.

You could say to him: Things are really lovely, so why rock the boat? On the other hand, you are 15 years further down the line: you have both gained your independence, you no longer have the worries of bringing up a family, you have had time and space to decide what you want. Don't be rushed into anything. He isn't going anywhere and it is obvious that he wants to be with you. Take your time, enjoy what you have, and be happy.

Q.4 I am desperately unhappy with a man who is violent and beats me and I have tried for years to leave him. I have collected bits of furniture which my sister has stored in her garage and I have found a flat. With a pension to come when I retire next month I feel I could have the peace and safety I desperately need. The problem is I am a Christian and I did promise to stay with my husband until death parted us. Am I right after 40 years to leave this man?

No one should have to live in a violent relationship and many would have given up sooner. You have given 40 years to this man and now it is time for you to feel safe. Take your chance and don't feel guilty. Pray that he will lose his violent temper and be able to find peace in his life as well.

Even if you are happy now, it pays to talk so that nothing spoils what you have together. If you are unhappy, what better time to try and change things. Remember that the man or woman you fell in love with may be older, they may have changed over the years but then so have you. Do you need to make more of an effort? Are you putting all the blame on to your partner?

Look closely at your chart. Even encourage your partner to do one as well. It is never too late to try to make things better, but it will take compromises on both sides. It won't be easy, it may be very hard, but the alternative is to do nothing and go into retirement unhappy, and that is quite scary. You may want to talk things through together or get counselling from Relate. Whichever you choose, you will be giving yourself the best basis for retirement, whether you have already retired or whether it is yet to come. Don't shut your eyes to the problems and pretend – you both deserve to be happy.

3

Hang on to those dreams

Don't dread being retired!

I can remember as a teenager I thought anyone over the age of 30 was well and truly past it, and when you reached 50 . . . well . . . was there really life after this? As for retirement, this seemed like something from another planet that I need not bother with. I looked at my grandparents who had settled into a quiet, rather dull day-to-day existence, hardly ever going out and certainly never going on holiday, and the thought of reaching that age didn't appeal at all.

As we all know, we grow up and each age has its drawbacks and compensations. From teenage years through romance, marriage and the struggle of getting a home together, to the day your own teenagers drive you mad, then you watch them proudly as they make their own way in life.

Out of all of life's stages, none can have changed so much as the retirement years. If I were a teenager now, what a different impression I would have. People in this stage of their life no longer even look like the grandparents I grew up with. You only have to look at the way they dress. With the family grown up, fewer worries about being there for everyone else, they wear nice clothes, have good hair-styles and look younger, happier and fitter than my grandparents ever did.

Talking about fitness: today's opportunities for keeping fit for the retired are endless. No longer the gentle walk their predecessors made do with. Aerobics, keep fit, step, ballet, aqua aerobics and tap-dancing classes are bursting at the seams with men and women often into their seventies and eighties. Add to this the number of people who play squash, badminton, golf or tennis, who swim, jog or go long-distance running, and it is plain to see that retired people are an age-group to be reckoned with in the fitness stakes. If there is a mountain to be scaled, a river to be fished or a play to be produced, you can bet your life it is a task one of them will be keen to take on because they have the time, the patience and life's experiences to help them do it.

Anyone who tells you life is dull after retirement has to be joking if my mailbag is anything to go by! All retired people seem to be reinvesting in their lives. They have renewed energy, an abundance of things they want to do, and often for the first time in their lives they can put themselves first. Many travel extensively, but even those who can't afford to travel find joy in visiting local beauty spots and often get involved in local conservation matters. Many decide to retrain, join the University of the Third Age or take an Open University degree.

Your expectations of retirement

What is important as you reach your retirement is your whole attitude to it. Be gloomy about it and that sums up what you can expect – dull endless hours wondering what it is all about. Think positively and you will probably drive your family mad because they will never know what you are up to next or where to find you. At least you won't be a burden, and you won't be boring either!

Let's now get down to the nitty gritty. Be honest with yourself. What are your expectations of retirement? Do you stop yourself thinking about it, convincing yourself that you don't need to worry about it until it happens? Are you scared stiff because you like life the way it is and you don't want it to change? Do you fear getting old and dying? Or are you bursting with enthusiasm and full of dreams that you want to fulfil? Maybe you are a bit of each of these. The important thing is to be honest with yourself. Don't cheat on your future – there is a lot at stake. Honesty about your emotions now will be an investment in the future, not a sign of weakness or over-exuberance. Maybe you should stop reading now and reflect on what I have said before returning to read on.

> Close your eyes . . . let yourself relax and look for the gate in your mind that you will soon go through into retirement. Does it seem to be surrounded by darkness or mist, or is there a nice warm light around it? This will give you a good indication about how you are feeling. It doesn't matter which it is . . . nothing is carved in stone . . . anything you want along the path of retirement can be changed. If you have negative thoughts about your retirement, don't worry, we will look at ways of dispersing these later in the chapter. Relax now and give yourself time to think . . .

Welcome back . . .

Now that you have returned to this book let us look at each of the feelings mentioned above in more detail.

We all like to feel comfortable with the way our lives are, but this feeling of comfort is something that comes about because of the familiar things that are around us and the way we have structured our lives. We mould our lives and fill our days with routines, family, friends and treats. When we feel comfortable with our lives, we are at one with ourselves and the world. You can liken this to those old shoes you continue to wear that fit with ease and never make your feet ache. They fit well, we like them . . . time for the dustbin? . . . No, there is plenty of wear in them yet!

Well, that is how giving up one way of life for another can feel. You get used to being at work with status, friends, colleagues and responsibilities. You may get fed up at times but what you know feels secure and much safer than stepping into the unknown.

No one says you have to look forward to retirement. There are no set rules that say you have to switch off your working mode and turn into a different type of person the day after your job comes to an end.

If you are scared stiff at the thought of retirement, that's OK, admit it. If you are not sure, then ask yourself the following questions:

- Am I blocking out thoughts of retirement?
- Will I miss my work and my friends?
- Do I worry how I will fill all those extra hours?
- Am I telling people I am looking forward to retirement because it is inevitable or because it is what people expect me to say?

Stepping into retirement is like sailing uncharted seas and you would have to be a robot to be totally bereft of any scared feelings – even if it is a slight niggle that you choose to ignore. Some scared feelings are perfectly normal and you don't have to push them away or feel guilty about them. Far better to accept the way you are and deal with these feelings as you go along.

The main thing to remember is that these scared feelings are pointers to areas that you are uncertain about – rather like an early-warning system. This is good because it gives you the opportunity to look at the things that might cause you problems rather than find yourself stranded and unhappy at a later date. Don't ignore these feelings – work on them!

Write down how you feel and try to analyse what you are worried about. Only when you can identify possible problems can you pave the way and prevent them. If you find writing things down a chore, and many people do, try talking into a cassette player instead. Choose a time when you can sit quietly. Switch on the cassette recorder, close your eyes, breathe deeply and slowly for a few moments, and relax.

Then start by saying who you are, what job you do, when you are going to retire and how you feel about retirement. Do it slowly and just ramble. Make sure you have a C90 tape so that there is no pressure on you to hurry. This will then give you 45 minutes each side. You don't have to think up clever or clear statements; just say the first thing that comes into your head. If you feel angry, be angry. If you feel sad, be sad.

Once you get going you will be surprised how easy it is. The first time you play back the tape you will probably think 'What a muddle . . . I sound like an idiot who can't string words together'. But when you listen to it a second or third time a few days apart you will begin to understand how you feel and the things that make you scared. You may want to repeat the process a couple more times. Each time you make a tape or list the things that scare you, you will become clearer and more able to focus on them and to work out ways of dealing with problems or prevent them arising in the first place.

Share your feelings

Keeping worries to yourself is the first pitfall you want to avoid. Remember, there are no prizes for battling on alone or putting on a brave face and trying to convince everyone that you are longing for retirement if that is not the way you feel. Talk to family, friends, colleagues and your employer. They can't help you if they don't know how you are honestly feeling. Finding out that your friends are equally scared at the prospect of retirement, or sharing their experiences, can help. Even if you don't like what you hear, at least you can make up your mind that this is one path you are not going down!

You can't blame an employer, who may have another 15 years before he or she has to retire, for thinking you can't wait to get off the work treadmill. If you tell them you are worried about being without a job they just might be able to offer you temporary or part-time employment after your retirement date. Also offer to come in as holiday or sick relief.

Any scared feelings must be honestly shared with your partner. Now is not the time to shut down on communication or try to allay any fears he or she might have by rushing off each Sunday hunting around car-boot sales for second-hand golf clubs or fishing lines! Buy your golf clubs by all means, but tell your partner how you feel. They are probably worried about the changes your retirement is going to make to their life and would welcome the opportunity to voice their fears.

There will be more chance of a happy and fulfilled retirement if you can have a positive approach and clear away as many doubts and fears as you can.

The fear of life coming to an end and dying also comes into play at this time. Dreadful sayings like 'waiting to die', 'the years between the golden handshake and the golden gates', 'one foot in the grave', 'on the scrap heap' and 'the wrinkle years' are often bandied about. Maybe in fun, but to those approaching retirement they can stick in the mind like thorns. Try to replace them with 'Tomorrow is the start of the rest of my life' – a good maxim to go to sleep on whatever your age.

The only certain thing we know when we are born is that one day we are going to die. There is no avoiding this. We don't know the day or the time, but one day it will come. Accept this and then get on with your life.

As a nation we are terrible at thinking about death let alone talking about it. How many times have you heard people say 'If I die'. Who are they kidding? Only themselves. Your life expectancy may be less now that you have reached retirement age, but you could live to be 104 – my nan did! Her husband died when she was 40, so she was a widow for 64 years and a pensioner for 44 of these. Thank goodness she got on with her life and didn't worry about when the fateful day would arrive – it would have been a long time to wait and worry. She did office cleaning until she was in her eighties and until her late nineties lived a very active life. She was always visiting people and it was hard to find her in.

Days may seem more precious once you retire. Spend them well and fill them with happiness. Don't spend your time waiting for death to arrive.

Finally, to those of you who are full of enthusiasm and bursting with dreams and ideas, good on you! Don't let anyone drag you down. Just be honest and sure that you are not putting on an act to cushion yourself. Clear up any little niggles. Even the happiest of retired people will say they had to make adjustments and compromises. Having said this, hang on to those dreams, they are what beautiful days are made of!

Postbag

Q.1 I thought I was looking forward to my retirement, but with only two weeks to go I am having grave doubts. My job involves a lot of responsibility and long hours. I have a team of people who report to me and I travel abroad twice a year on business. With an expense account I also eat out a lot. I play golf and squash when I have time. It has suddenly hit me that life is going to be pretty dull after all this.

Different maybe, dull no. You have the qualities that many organizations are crying out for. If money is not too much of a problem then you could be a boon to a small business who needs your professional skills on a part-time basis, or to one of the many voluntary organizations who need people with managerial skills like yours. There must be many things that you never had time to do. Now is the chance to make up for lost time.

Q.2 I retired four weeks ago having been in a job I hated for 30 years. I thought retirement would be more than welcome. Instead I find I am restless and can't focus on anything, even though I have many things I want to do. A friend suggests I might be depressed but I don't think I am. Like many situations in life, retirement takes time to settle into. Four weeks is not long to unpick the threads of a working life, even one you didn't like, and begin to weave a new life. Take each day as it comes. If you can achieve one of your goals from time to time, that's great, but if not, don't worry. Let things roll and gradually your life will settle into place. If you are worried you might be depressed see your doctor and get your mind put at rest.

Q.3 As a single woman I have always lived with my brother who is very selfish. Whilst both worked, it was impossible to get him to help in the house. I worked full time and did everything. When he retired four years ago I insisted he did the cleaning as he was home all day. I retire soon and he has told a friend he can't wait for this as he won't have to do any more housework. I am tired. I don't want to spend my retirement looking after him and the house, but I know he will be difficult if I don't.
Listen, be a doormat and he will walk all over you! He has no right to expect you to look after him or take on all the housework when you retire, and the sooner you tell him this the better. If he won't continue to clean the house tell him he can do his own washing, cooking and ironing – and mean it!

Q.4 My wife and I made many plans for our retirement. We would buy the bungalow we had always dreamed of and live there in the summer and go to Spain in the winter, we even got as far as looking at bungalows a few months before I retired. Then out of the blue she told me there was someone else in her life and had been for 13 years. She hadn't seen him for six months as she had made up her mind she wanted to stay with me, but now she had changed her mind and would be moving out. I watched in a daze as she packed, asking if she could take this or that. I didn't know or care about the things in our home, I just knew I didn't want her to go. I begged and I pleaded, but to no avail. She took very little and wants nothing from me, she has filed for divorce and they are buying a house in France. Friends say I should forget her and try to get on with my life. My employers have suggested that I stay on for another three years instead of taking the early retirement I had requested and I have done this. My life and all the dreams I had, winters in the sun, are shattered and I don't know what to do with my life.
You are having to cope with the loss of everything you held dear and the realization that you have been deceived for such a long time. This won't

be easy. I think you have done the right thing in agreeing to stay at work, this will give your life some stability. Don't abandon your plans to live abroad, these are your dreams. Three years is a long time now until you retire, much can happen and you may find someone else to share your dreams with . . . I hope so.

Q.5 It has always been my ambition to travel around the world when I retired. To take as much as I could carry and set off. My wife died ten years ago and I have been very lonely since then. My children are married, I am comfortably off and there seemed nothing to stop me. Now that the time has come, at 65 I am wondering if I am being a silly old fool. Friends wish me luck but I sense that they think I am strange to be doing this. My family back me but wish I wasn't going alone, asking what would happen if I became ill. Being fit and healthy, I hadn't given this much thought, but now I do. Am I being stupid and irresponsible?
Quite the reverse! Pack your bits and bobs and go. If you don't, you will always regret it. You may set off alone but I am certain you will meet a lot of people along the way and make some really good friends. When you set off, the world will probably seem a very big place, but gradually as you travel around it will seem to get smaller. At the very worst you can always come back; at best the places you visit and the people you meet will enrich the rest of your life.

I once heard someone say her parents spent their retirement always looking back and hankering for the past. So much so she dreaded retiring herself. Then to her surprise she found it was quite the reverse. She is so busy she is constantly looking forward and planning her days. There certainly isn't time to keep looking back. I think this sums up the differences in attitude you can have. Get a positive attitude and emotionally you will cope. Even if you have already retired and you feel emotionally drained it is not too late. No one says you have to have everything cut and dried on the day you retire – very few people do. Whether you are weeks, months or years into your retirement you can still take stock and alter your attitude and path.

Once again use a tape. Describe how you wanted your retirement to be, how it has turned out and what upsets or disappoints you. Go on to describe how you would like to change your retirement. Listen to the tape several times, then make up your mind to be positive. Look in a mirror each day. Tell yourself: 'I deserve to be happy and intend to be.'

33

Gradually you will believe this, and as your attitude changes so will your emotions. You will also notice a change for the better in your appearance. Tension will ease, a softer look will appear and you may be surprised to see that you look younger. What we feel inside radiates through.

4
To work or not to work?

Am I staying in bed too long in the morning? Does my day lack a purpose to encourage me to get up? Do I miss some of the things I complained about when I did go out to work? Do I lack a driving force in my life?

If the answer to most of these questions is yes then maybe it is time to consider going back to work part time, either in a paid or voluntary capacity. With 2,000 extra hours to fill each year, many people find time hangs heavily on their hands, especially if they are living alone or have few interests.

When you think about it, in your life your whole upbringing and education have been telling you you need to get a job. You may now realize you miss your colleagues and the teamwork. If you were a workaholic, saying goodbye to your firm may have left you feeling insecure. If you thought you were indispensable, it may have come as a dreadful shock to realize they were willing to let you go and that some bright spark was waiting in the wings to take your place.

Also you have to remember that the first few months of retirement are pretty easy to fill. But once you have decorated the house, done all the DIY chores, made the homemade cakes and wines, got the garden in tiptop shape, painted the gate, given the drains a surprise when you got down and cleaned them, and got the windows cleaner than they had ever been, you may run out of things to keep you occupied.

Working after retirement

At this point, a lot of you may throw your hands up in horror and say you don't want to get back into the rat race. Well, read on for a while, because that is not what I am suggesting for one moment. Going back to work full time seems to me to be a pretty silly thing to do, after all you need time to build up other interests for when you get older and may not be fit enough to work. Some people retire and immediately get another full time job only to have to go through the whole retirement bit again some years later!

What I am suggesting is part-time work which gives you a sense of purpose but still allows plenty of time for other things. If money is short, paid work will be preferable, whether you find any will very much depend upon your attitude and expectations. Some professions such as accountancy, teaching and catering can lead on quite easily to part-time freelance work. For instance, there are many small businesses who cannot afford a large firm of accountants to do their books; having an experienced accountant who is willing to take on several customers at a reasonable rate may suit clients and retired accountants alike. Private tuition for those who are studying for their exams, or extra help for those studying English or Maths might also be required by many students. Those in the catering profession often set up on their own after retirement or find part-time work quite easily. Some careers are far too technical or specialized for people to find part-time work in a similar line. This means rethinking what other work you would be willing to take.

The good thing about working after retirement is that emotionally it is in most cases far less stressful. You are working because you want to, not because you have to. If you don't like a job, or you find it takes up too much of your time, you can give it up and be more selective. Before retirement there may be many stresses and strains attached to the job you did, but you probably had to stick it out because of your mortgage, the family and your pension. Because of these ties life may have become a drudge and made you feel tense and irritable because you had no choice other than to keep going.

Now you do have choices:

- whether you work or not
- who you work for
- where you work
- what you are prepared to work for
- how long you work
- when you work.

You can also have 'ideals' when choosing work. You may want to work with the sick and disabled, or work voluntarily for a cause that is close to your heart. You may want to get involved with a political party whose views you want to take further. You may want to give your time to a Citizens Advice Bureau, Victim Support Group, or become a Samaritan or Relate counsellor.

What matters most when it comes to making decisions as to whether you should work or not is the quality of your life. If you feel a job would improve it, then go for it. Some might ask how we define the quality of our life. Well, apart from the materialistic things that tend to make life harder or easier for us, we will be looking at our inner soul and inner warmth. Although what makes for contentment varies from one person to another, I think we all know the feeling of 'all is right with the world and me'. Sometimes it takes a lot to make us feel this way, other times just a glance, smile or a simple act will make us glow inside, and this radiates to our face and on to others.

Getting a job

Many people feel that once the label 'retired' has been stamped on them the chance of getting work diminishes. To a certain extent they are right; employers' attitudes often reflect old-fashioned views that once retired you are well and truly past it. As many of these employers are in their thirties and forties I suppose to them retirement age does seem old.

If you want to continue working I think you have to do two things. First, change these attitudes, and, second, let it be known before you retire that you will be looking for work before that label gets stuck on you. Changing attitudes may seem a hard task and you can't hope to do this across the board, but what you can do is change the attitude of anyone who interviews you or who you write to for a job. It is a very simple process and I have seen it work many times. If you think your age may be against you, then make a list of all the reasons why you should be employed. This would include:

- I will bring enthusiasm to the job. I will be doing it because I want to, not like many younger employees who have to.
- Life has taught me to value myself, and therefore I place a high value on any jobs that I do.
- As a mature person I am reliable; I am not going to have to take time off to have children, to look after them when they are sick or on holiday.
- I am not going to have a day off because I am upset at having fallen out with one of my latest boyfriends or girlfriends.
- Older peoples' timekeeping is usually good.
- Because money is not the prime consideration for me working, my employer will know I am doing the job because I enjoy it.
- I have a wide range of skills to take to a job. (Add your personal ones to this list.)

When you have done this, include these reasons in your application or letter, even enclose a photograph of yourself, preferably smiling. When your application lands on a prospective employer's desk you want it to stand out against the rest. It has to be concise as he or she won't want to spend hours ploughing through it. If you can get the attention of the employer in the first sentence so that they go on to read your reasons why at retirement age you should be employed, you will stand a good chance of making them stop and consider what you are saying and may change their attitudes to employing a retired person.

Some employers actually make a conscious effort to employ retired people. Many supermarkets realize the potential and reliability of this age group. They are just one sector who are tapping into this valuable part of the workforce.

Starting a business

Not everyone wants to work for someone else. Some retired people see this as a golden opportunity to realize their ambition and work for themselves. When it happens they find real satisfaction and a sense of achievement that may have escaped them all their working lives.

Take the story of Edward. He had dabbled in magic tricks since he was a boy. When he grew older and had a family of his own Christmas and birthdays were never complete without Edward's magic act. The family knew the tricks inside out but still cheered every time. When Edward retired from being a carpet salesman he knew he wanted to do something with his time, but he didn't know what. He is a member of a social club and one afternoon, when a pianist failed to turn up to entertain a group of elderly people, he stepped in with his box of tricks. Amazed at the response he got he decided to try and fill some of his time and earn a little bit of money this way. With Christmas approaching he soon found he was booked three or four times a week as word spread. The highlight for him that year was Christmas Eve, when he entertained the children who had to stay in the local hospital. He says he will never forget it. With his family around him he felt he had found something in his life that not only brought him happiness but others as well. 'I saw the childrens' faces,' he told me, 'and I knew I was doing the right thing.' He never charges charities, children's homes or elderly people's homes, and charges only a small amount for private functions. He and his wife recently had a weekend away with what he had saved from doing his shows. 'That's a bonus,' he told me, 'it's the happiness it brings that counts the most.'

If you drive, then the possibilities for working are good, shops often want deliveries done and car hire firms are always looking for careful drivers. Female drivers are in demand as many women don't like going in cars driven by men, particularly in the evening.

If you enjoy cooking the opportunities are also there. Catering for weddings or companies is covered by the large caterers, but what about those who can't afford this? There are many young couples getting married on a budget and small firms who can't afford to get big caterers in. This is where you can corner the undeveloped area of the market. Determination must be your password. Banish the words 'can't' and 'but' from your vocabulary and you will be half way there. Without the large overheads many companies have, you will probably find you can produce less fancy but good quality cakes and buffets at a price that suits you both. Cards in windows are an investment and a leaflet drop in your local area will help. For those who don't like cooking, what about a sandwich round? Many offices are some distance from the shops and would welcome a regular daily delivery of sandwiches, crisps, cakes, biscuits and cold drinks. Do remember before you get carried away on the crest of all this enthusiasm to check with the Health and Safety people at your local Council about the Safety Regulations governing the production of food from home.

If you enjoy gardening this can also lead to employment. So can painting, decorating, plumbing and electrical work. If you enjoy viewing houses why not do as Margaret does? She works for an Estate Agent on Sundays taking people at prearranged times to view houses. This means the regular staff get a day off and the Sunday employee who works in the office doesn't have to shut up shop to go out on appointments.

Finally, let me tell you about Christine, who had never worked. She had brought up five children and has nine grandchildren all scattered across the country. Until her husband died she was quite happy to be at home. After he died she felt trapped with nowhere to go. She set about getting a job but didn't think she had anything to offer.

Some months after her husband's death she was having coffee with her next-door neighbour, a young woman with twin girls of six. She told Christine it was the twins' birthday the following Sunday and she was dreading the party, 'hard work' was how she described it. Christine offered to help. The day arrived and her neighbour had a tummy bug, the party would have to be cancelled. Not so, because Christine did it with a little help from the twins' dad, who decided the safest place was the kitchen doing the washing up. If I can do it once I can do it again, decided Christine, and she did. Now known as 'Christine the party lady' she has at least two parties a week; the only thing the parents have to do is provide the food. She brings the puppets, music, sweets, prizes and arranges games before tea and entertains the children, with them participating, afterwards. She only does it for children up to the age of eight; after this she says she leaves it to the disco organizers or the parents to organize outings. Children over eight get bored with games, and that's not what parties are about – they must be fun.

So you see, it is possible to make a business out of the simplest thing, provided you are in the right frame of mind. We all have things we dislike doing, it may be cleaning or the ironing, for others it could be doing the VAT returns. These are tasks people will willingly pay to have done for them. Does someone want to have their phone calls transferred to you as an answering service so that they don't lose work and clients don't have to talk to an answer phone machine?

From bed and breakfast to consultancy work, or baby-sitting to freelance journalism, or from holiday pet-caring to running a PR company. These are all businesses that retired people have written to me saying they have set up from home since retiring, and with very little financial outlay. You could do it too; be positive and give it a try. The emotional reward, satisfaction and achievement far outweigh any initial worries. And if you don't like it, you can pack it up and try something different. Retirement gives you choices – not dead-end jobs.

Helping others

If voluntary work appeals to you, then the possibilities are endless. The library holds a directory of all voluntary services with hundreds of voluntary agencies who need help.

It is important at this stage to look at your reasons for wanting to do voluntary work. If you are on a do-gooder trail, then stop and think again. A lot of people you may come into contact with are going to be vulnerable and may lack self-confidence due to their situation. The last thing they need is someone who comes in doing the 'bountiful act'. Voluntary work has to be a two-way thing. Yes, you will be giving some much-needed help, but you too can get a lot from it. It will give you satisfaction, but also see it as a learning curve in your life. Listen to the people you come in contact with and learn from their experiences. You may see sadness, pain and heartache, but you will also see kindness, stamina and courage. No one ever knows everything or is too old to learn.

Although it is nice to earn money for work done, it can sometimes put restrictions on what you can do. For instance, a wage tag will usually mean you are paid to do a certain job within certain parameters. Voluntary work is extremely valued and therefore a certain amount of choice as to what you do comes with it. We keep talking about choices and I make no apologies for this because I think it is the difference between working life before retirement and afterwards. You now have choices and will feel differently about your work.

It's your choice

It is a fact of life that very few people do a job during their working life that they really enjoy. Most do it to pay the bills and look after their families. Some jobs are more tolerable than others and will probably affect your decision as to whether you work after retirement or not.

Let me tell you about Bill, who worked on an assembly line ten hours a day for over 40 years. He told me he got no satisfaction from his job whatsoever. He could do it with his eyes closed and was often tempted to try but didn't. It was repetitive, boring and soul-destroying. He needed the money and stuck it out. Only workmates made it bearable.

The day after retirement he couldn't believe he didn't have to get up and go to the factory again. It took months and several attacks of nerves for him to get over the strain he had been working under all those years. Today he sells teas, snacks and ice-creams from a mobile tea van in a busy lay-by on a rural country route. The many lorry drivers who stop each day remind him of what used to be, then he looks at the countryside around him and the families who stop on the way to the coast and is glad he is 'sort of' retired.

Pam worked as a music teacher all her life. She travelled in this country and abroad with talented students as they took part in competitions and concerts across Europe. When retirement age came she left the boarding-school she worked for and bought a cottage nearby in the West Country. Her biggest worry was that she would be lonely as she is single and has no family. To begin with she did some piano and violin lessons, but as these tied her to the cottage for a large proportion of the afternoons and evenings, she decided to quit and retire completely. She joined a local conservation group and the WI, and took up painting at a local art group. Here she met Roy, a retired naval officer who had never married. Five years on they were married and Roy discovered he had a daughter he never knew about from a relationship 24 years ago. They paint, they sail, they see 'their' daughter, son-in-law and grandson. Life is good . . . and they certainly don't want to work.

When there is an age gap in a marriage, one partner will probably continue working long after the other. This can cause problems, especially if it is the woman who continues to work. It has to be said that a lot of people equate work with their status in the community. When this is taken away they can feel worthless.

When Phil, now aged 68, retired, his wife Anne was 47. The children had not long left home and she was eager to launch herself on a career. Having worked some years back on a national newspaper as a freelance writer, she had little difficulty getting work on a local daily newspaper. She was over the moon. Deputy Features Editor on a reasonable salary and she looked forward to a promising career. Within a year she was back on a national newspaper. Phil had also been a journalist, but on television; he was forced to take retirement, not only because of his age but also his health wouldn't stand all the travelling the job involved.

As Anne's career flourished, so Phil's self-esteem diminished. He became moody and aggressive, and accused her of having an affair when a deadline kept her late. He wouldn't consider any other work and started drinking. Their marriage, now shaky, took a downward turn when Anne found he was having an affair. They separated for a month and then Anne returned on the understanding that he would go to Alcoholics Anonymous and they would both go to Relate for counselling. In the end he did neither and they divorced.

Colin and Eve, on the other hand, talked through the problems that could arise before he retired. At 63 he took early retirement and together with a friend rented a shop that sold anything and everything for £1 an item. Meanwhile, Eve, at 45, had got herself a major promotion in the PR company where she worked. There was no animosity between them; Colin loved his easy-going job and saw it as a challenge to get as many different and unusual items that he could into the shop. He was pleased for Eve, but didn't envy her being up there in what he termed 'the rat race'.

Finally, we look at Melvin and Betty. Neither wanted full- or part-time jobs, but both wanted an antique shop. Unfortunately, without the cash this scheme has not been realized. Instead they have a market stall on Wednesdays and Saturdays and go to several car-boot sales to look for items for their stall every Sunday. Not only profitable, but fun as well.

Not everyone wants to work after retirement. If you are happy at home that is fine. So long as you have other interests that stop you becoming a vacuum cleaner or cobweb fanatic with very little else to do or talk about, then forget about work if you want to. If money is short and you need to work, don't overdo it, and try to find something that you enjoy.

Finally, a word of warning about franchises. A franchise involves buying into an idea, package or company, such as a restaurant or dry-cleaning business, where you have to run it on the company's terms. You may also have to pay a percentage of your profits to them. Some are good and perfectly above board, others more dubious, as several letters to me have reported. It is easy to become despondent if you want a job and can't find one and feel you want to be your own boss in a franchise. Before parting with a penny, speak to your bank and your solicitor.

Postbag

Q.1 My husband has retired and is quite happy to be at home. As an ex-nurse I have seen what can result when men give up, sit in armchairs watching television and become old men quicker than they should. I retired six years ago and although I don't work I have a very active life – lots of clubs, friends and social events. Does it sound right in wanting him to get a part-time job?

Be honest about your reasons, then talk to him. I agree that some may give up and sit and watch television all day but I am not entirely satisfied if this is all that is bothering you. You have had the house to yourself for several years, are you getting fed up with having him around all the time? Whatever the reason, you need to talk and sort things out honestly before there is a real problem.

Q.2 My ex-employer has contacted me and asked if I would like to do consultancy work for the company. Although I am flattered to be asked I am not sure I want to work, but if I give up this opportunity I won't be asked again. I retired four weeks ago.

Had this offer come further into your retirement you might have felt differently. At the moment you are a bit like a schoolboy let out at the end of term and enjoying your summer holiday. Find out the extent of the work that is on offer. Consultancy work is often part time and in chunks rather than continuous days or weeks. Decide how much time you might be prepared to give, perhaps one or two days a week, and offer this. It sounds as if they need you and will probably be willing to negotiate. It might be worth giving it a try. After all, you can always change your mind at a later date and give it up.

Q.3 I had a small part-time job as a daytime security clerk, now they have decided to do away with this post and I am at home with the wife all the time. She likes me to be around and gives me lots of jobs to do. I have never been the domesticated type of man and I hate this. I feel patronized. I want to find another job but she keeps telling me that at 67 I won't.

If you don't want to be at home, then with determination I think you will find a job. You are one of the more fortunate men whose wife wants you to be around. This really is an advantage and reassurance for when the time comes and you don't want to work. Don't turn your back completely on domesticity; all men should know how to cook and look after the home in case their partner is sick or they are ever alone.

Q.4 My husband and I own a small but busy newsagent's in North Wales. We have been doing this for 30 years and are not ready to give up yet. Our children, however, think we should as we are both 70 this year. They say we never have time for anything else other than work because we open seven days a week. We have two half days off, and have talked about it, but we like our life the way it is. The children are becoming more persistent and we don't want to fall out with them. How can we get them to understand that we are happy the way things are?

Working seven days a week is a lot for anyone. I also wonder if you are getting up exceedingly early each day to mark up the papers and this is what worries them. The old saying 'all work and no play is no good for you' is true – the balance has to be right. Emotionally your shop is important to you, so carry on for as long as you want. Your children are showing love and concern; they may also want a bit more of your time. If you can let go of the reins and let someone else run the shop at least one day a week, your family would see more of you and you might find you enjoy time off.

Whether you decide to try and get a job or not, or hope you will find your retirement fulfilling, never sell yourself short and remember retirement is about making your own decisions and choices. You don't have to do what someone else tells you any more.

5

When am *I* going to retire?

Although times are changing and many women now go out to work, there are still situations where the woman has been at home all her life whilst the man worked. Trying to adjust to having her partner around is hard for many women.

When you have had your time and the house to yourself for many years, it can come as a bit of a shock to find your partner is with you almost 24 hours a day. The man that came home at six, ate dinner, watched television, went to bed only to return to his place of work the next day, may seem a far cry from the man who is now with you all the time. 'Did I really look forward to the weekends when he didn't have to work?' you might ask yourself. Feeling dreadfully guilty for even letting such a thought creep into your mind you go on to ask 'Is this the same man I have been living with for all those years? Am I going to be able to stand having him around all the time? Will our relationship survive this new togetherness? Do I want it to? Am I mean for even thinking this way?' The answer to the last question first: no, you are not, so stop feeling guilty!

Let me let you into a little secret. The very first letter I ever received as an agony aunt was from a woman whose husband had retired. She told me she had dreaded him retiring because she valued having time to do the things she wanted on her own, her 'selfish time' she called it. When she said goodbye to him when he went to work she revelled in the peaceful atmosphere of the house and the day ahead to fill as she pleased.

She couldn't bear the thought of him being around, and at the same time she felt disloyal for having these feelings. At my suggestion she told her husband. At first he was hurt and very much on the defensive, but talking brought out his fears about retirement, as well as hers. She learnt that he was frightened at the prospect of having so much time on his hands and that he might quickly age after retirement. Together they planned his retirement so that they could keep their individuality, have their own space and enjoy a good relationship.

We all change

Now let us look at how you feel at the moment and the thoughts going through your mind. Let's start with the first thing on our list. Is he the

45

same man you have lived with all these years? Well, I suppose the truthful answer will have to be 'Yes and no'. Throughout life we gather and discard information, attitudes, emotions, thoughts and feelings. These are ever-changing – or, at least, should be! People who stand still don't grow emotionally, don't move eagerly from one stage in life to another, and feel alienated at times. Retirement will bring changes emotionally and it would be silly to try and avoid this. Yes, he will be different, but so will you.

The 'no' will represent the man you set out with, the man you fell in love with and whom you wanted to spend the rest of your life with. No, deep down you won't change his basic good points, and the things that irritate will still be there, but now you may perceive them in a completely different way. For example, retirement won't alter a partner's pedantic or stingy nature but it may make it harder to live with. At the other end of the scale, having someone with a generous nature won't change once retirement comes, but they may decide to channel this energy in a different way and to other sources than just you and your family. For instance, they might take up voluntary work.

Life shouldn't be seen as static, it should be like a river that winds and flows, sometimes still, and at other times fast and wild. Like a river it will have bends and we won't know what lies ahead. It could be a beautiful setting or it could be bleak. Life is ever-changing, like the moulding and meandering of the river, and we can shape the river of our lives.

Are you going to be able to stand having him around all the time? My mailbag suggests it is necessary to make adjustments and talk to avoid tearing your hair out. Remember what I told you about adjusting to being a parent? You had to make changes, but you didn't do it without a lot of planning. Remember the plans that you sat talking over night after night: what name for the baby, what kind of parents you wanted to be, how you would cope with the strain it would put on your relationship. It's back to the drawing board and good old planning again! Say how you feel, work out time for yourself and things you want to do alone and things you want to do together.

Two's company?

Togetherness works for some people, but for others it can be the kiss of death to a relationship. Let me tell you the tale of a woman whose kitchen was haunted by what appeared to be an invisible pair of hands after her husband retired.

Taps that had been left running at the sink to wash salads were switched off, cakes half baked were suddenly deprived of heat because the phantom hands had switched the power off at the wall. Household items that had stood quite happily in one place for years were suddenly moved as part of the great reorganization that the hands had planned. The final straw came when opening the washing machine one day. This poor woman was hit by a torrent of soapy water – why, for goodness sake, had the machine stopped in the middle of the cycle, another plug switched off! By now I am sure you will have guessed that it was not a ghostly phantom – it was her husband who was going around switching plugs off, as he termed, 'for safety reasons and to save money'. Did she need to wash salads under running water? he asked. How was he to know when the washing machine was at a standstill it was resting between washing cycles? Waste of time, he described it. As for his reorganization plans, he thought he was helping her. Fortunately, he narrowly escaped violence when he told her she wasted more time than she spent productively, and the list that he had drawn up to help save time and money on the domestic chores went very rapidly into the dustbin.

However, he may have been trying in his own way to tell her he was worried about money now that he was retired.

Many people find living on a reduced income, especially when they have not had to worry before, puts a great strain on the relationship and can cause arguments. It is important to discuss this and come to a mid-way approach to expenditure: one that doesn't stretch the budget, but also one that doesn't go to the other extreme of becoming miserly. When you receive a lump sum on retirement it can seem as if you are well off. Arguments often come about when one partner wants to break into the capital and the other doesn't want to. Once again, talk about this. Don't spend, spend, spend, because you may need some money for a rainy day. On the other hand, retirement is about enjoying yourself, so don't stint on the occasional treat even if it may seem an extravagance.

Then there was the case of the husband who wanted to accompany his wife everywhere she went. He drove her not only to distraction but also to calculated and devious means. After eight weeks of never a moment apart, one morning she crept out to the garage, opened the garage doors, put her things in the car and left the car door open. She then made him a cup of coffee and as soon as he had settled down to drink it she said a quick 'goodbye, I'm off to the shops' and within seconds she was in the car and off. She explained it was the only way she could think of for getting some time on her own. On her return he was hurt and upset, but it gave her the opening to say how she felt. He then quickly moved on to 'you don't want me . . . I'm obviously in the way', the feeling-sorry-for-myself mode. At that precise moment he was right: she was fed up with him acting like a limpet; even when she went to the toilet he would call out and ask her where she was.

'If you prefer your friends to me . . .' is another phrase that drives women mad. They don't prefer friends to anything, they just enjoy the company of being with their friends, going to their women's groups, out for a day or just meeting for a coffee and a chat. Being asked to give these up when her husband retires often happens. Some wives do it and then are angry and miserable because of it. Others refuse but have to pay the price of sulks and bad moods for going. Have you ever looked out of your window and seen a bird sitting by the empty bird table hoping someone will put some food out? Well, that is how one woman described her husband, sitting there with his beak open, still geared to his working routine which had coffee breaks around 10 a.m. and 11.30 a.m., followed by lunch at 1 p.m. and tea at 3 p.m. He would hover in the kitchen doorway at these feeding times, or shift around in his chair, uneasily glancing at his watch as he did so. His wife, now thoroughly fed up with the whole thing, would ignore him. When his bowel habits changed, he couldn't contain his frustration any longer and as he went out of the door on his way to see the doctor he left her with this sobering comment: 'It's all your fault, my stomach is used to a routine.' 'So are my nerves,' she shouted back at him as he disappeared out of sight.

One extra meal a day might seem a small thing to some people to get upset about, but having to be around to get this meal when in the past the day was your own can seem a nightmare. Not only in practical terms, but emotional ones as well. 'He has taken over' is another regular cry, as is 'He makes the place untidy'. Taking the last statement first, having someone around all day who has no idea of the amount of extra work they generate when they leave coffee mugs by chairs, wet towels chucked willy-nilly in the bathroom, dirty clothes in corners and crumbs on tables and in grill pans, is the most irritating thing. Men tend to have a mental block where toilet rolls are concerned; when they are changed, men can seem totally incapable of throwing away the old cardboard toilet roll or the polythene cover of the new one. According to my postbag they are left on floors, cisterns and even in the sinks for that 'good natured bathroom fairy' to dispose of.

When it comes to 'taking over', this usually presents itself, as in one of our previous case histories, as time to bring into the home a new system designed to put the poor misguided wife on a more organized plane. The fact that she has run the home for 30 or 40 years seems totally irrelevant. Managerial and organizational skills from the husband's working life are champing at the bit for a new avenue to follow. So without further ado, what better place to start than the home? Surely she should be pleased that he had taken an interest? He can't understand why she is seething.

Coupled with the new organizing regime often comes the 'take-over bid'. Some women don't even realize it is happening until one day they wake up to find all the household decisions have been taken away from them. One man I heard of even tried to introduce a time and motion study into his wife's domestic day. Later, talking to his daughter who had given a temporary refuge to his fleeing wife, he said 'I was only trying to help', and probably he was.

From his point of view

Before we look at ways of avoiding and solving these problems, I think it is only fair to look at things from the man's point of view. Having worked for most of his life, approaching retirement can be viewed with varying emotions from 'can't wait' to 'oh my God, what will I do'. Even if men go on pre-retirement courses they are often totally unprepared for the emotional upheaval retirement can bring. One day they are working and probably part of a team, the next they have 2,000 hours a year ahead to fill. Is it any wonder that the first place they look at is the home? Having watched their wives do battle with the cooking and housework for years, and maybe heard endless complaints about having to do it all, many men genuinely feel they are doing the right thing by offering to help or by taking on some of the responsibility. Then they end up totally confused when they find not only is their help not welcome but they are accused of interfering, being a nuisance and totally insensitive.

Although many men long to leave their jobs and retire, very few actually consider how they are going to feel when they do it and how their wives will react. 'You never have time for me' is a cry heard from many women when their husbands are busy with their jobs. 'I now have more time for her, she will be pleased', the poor man kids himself when he retires. And what happens? She says she's sick of having him around under her feet all day. It seems he can't win. There are in fact no winners or losers in these situations, neither should there be. What is necessary is compromise on both sides so that retirement is an easy way of life rather than a breeding ground for resentments and arguments.

Occasionally one partner will be entirely happy with the way things are and totally oblivious to their partner's unhappiness, but in most cases, like the ones we have touched on, neither partner is happy; they are just existing, each doggedly hanging on to what makes them feel secure. The woman, although she may be hating the household chores, clings to them because they are things that give her life 'normality'. Give these up and she thinks she will be the one who feels all at sea. The man, on the other hand, has little or no choice in his change in circumstances, his 'life raft' is drifting and he needs a secure mooring for his time and energies.

A time to rethink

Whether you are approaching retirement, have just retired or have been retired for some time, if you recognize yourself in this chapter now is the time to rethink. For those with long-term difficulties, talk to your partner about your unhappiness. If this doesn't work I would strongly recommend counselling with Relate. Once you get locked into conflict over a number of years it is difficult to change things. Counselling can help unlock the situation and in doing so help you find mutual ground.

If your problems are anticipated or reasonably recent, then you should be able to work them out between you. Arrange to have some 'kind honesty' time. I put the word 'kind' in purposely because honesty can be brutal and it is not the route to take if you want to work this out. Try the following exercise.

Each make a list of things that bother you. Agree to talk to each other in an honest but kind way, taking it in turns for around two to three minutes each. That might sound short but it isn't really and it does stop you waffling and helps you keep to the point. Whilst one partner is talking the other should give their full attention without interrupting. When your partner finishes their turn you can respond and ask any questions. Allow up to an hour the first time you do this. If things get heated, agree to leave it and have another try the following day or week. When you do complete an hour, decide whether you need more time and agree when to have this.

If you both feel you have said everything that needs to be said, agree to each make a list of compromises and then talk these through using the same method.

For example, the man who kept turning the cooker and plugs off in the kitchen will hopefully realize that his well-intended time- and cost-cuts actually caused waste, damage and extra costs. His wife, on the other hand, doesn't realize he is worried about managing on a reduced income. Help that is interpreted as interfering needs to be reassessed. Very few wives like every domestic chore, stop feeling threatened and off-load some that you don't like on to him if that is what he wants. Does it really matter who vacuums or irons?

If your partner seems uncaring and you feel in her way, don't despair, talk about it, tell her you feel insecure or that you like being with her, but don't go into a huff when she says she needs to claim some space back. If you think about it, what will you talk about for the next 20 years or so if you never do anything apart? When you come to your session where you talk about compromise, work out the time you both have and divide it into three parts: time solely for each other, time doing hobbies and outings together, and time for your own pursuits. Take turns at housework, gardening and cooking ... and especially those cups of coffee and lunches. If you find your wife needs to be a bit more organized, please think before you say this. You may have held down a good job over the years but your wife has held down many tasks including housekeeping, childminding, counselling, budgeting, nursemaiding, to name but a few. In fact, she has been running a business – it's called 'Family & Home', no mean task: little, if any, salary, often on duty 24 hours a day, no days off and certainly no promotions! So try to understand if she is a bit touchy over your 'let's revolutionize the chores' manifesto!

Postbag

Q.1 I know it may sound awful but I am dreading my husband's retirement. I am used to having the home to myself and being able to come and go as I please. My husband talks about 'doing things together'. This worries me as I have my clubs that I like to go to and my friends who I like to see, I wouldn't want to give them up.

There is no need to give up anything when your husband retires. He needs to sort out the time you are going to spend together and the time you do things on your own. Togetherness is wonderful for some relationships but for others it is a total disaster and the relationship breaks up. There is no reason why you should have to give up your friends or your social activities but try to understand that retirement will be a new way of life for him and he may cling to you because he feels a bit insecure. Encourage him to find new interests in his life and to talk to you when he is feeling unhappy.

Q.2 When I retired I thought I would be able to help out in the house. I have tried this but it angered my wife, she said I was being bossy and trying to take over her role. It is my home as well and I only wanted to help. Where did I go wrong?

Be honest. Were you offering a helping hand or had you earmarked certain tasks to keep you occupied without asking your wife if she minded? Yes, it is your home but for years the running of it has been your wife's. Think how you might have felt if someone had come along and taken away part of your job when you were at work. Feelings of insecurity and irritation would possibly have crept in; you might even have wondered whether you were going to have to job share or be made redundant. Well, this is how your wife feels, she doesn't want her role eroded, she needs to feel useful. Ask your wife if there is anything you can do to help rather than jumping in. If she is adamant she doesn't want help, then you are going to have to look for other things to do, such as decorating, maintenance or working in the garden. Alternatively you could look for a part-time job or become involved in other things in the community.

Q.3 I am really worried about my parents. Dad retired a few months ago and their relationship has deteriorated. They used to have the odd tiff but the majority of the time they got on well. Now every time I go to see them they are bickering, often over petty little things. I can't believe they have got like this, both seem upset and fed up. What can I do?
You can be there for either of them if they want to talk but don't fall into the trap of taking sides. What you describe is very common especially within the first few months of retirement when settling into a new way of life. They have to find their own way and as much as you love them, if you interfere they won't thank you for it. Things might be easier if they had some time apart and you could encourage their individual interests without making decisions for them.

For you both to achieve harmony in your domestic arrangements it will mean give and take. For the woman, yes, you may have had your home to yourself for all those years. Well, think yourself lucky, now is the time to share, it's his home too! For the male partner who has previously been out to work, you know this is or was a sensitive area, so tread carefully. Think how you would have felt on the shop floor or in your office if a new bod had come along and tried to alter things. Wouldn't your hackles rise? Wouldn't you think, what a cheek, who do they think they are?

Unhappiness is often caused by resentment, resentment comes about through angry feelings; angry feelings come about because we feel things are not fair; unfairness occurs through thoughtless actions; thoughtless actions through lack of understanding and lack of communication. So we come back not only to talking to each other but, just as importantly, listening to what our partner is saying. Only then is there any hope of reaching the right emotional balance that is needed to live together for those extra 2,000 hours each year.

6
Itchy feet?

Whether you want to move to that cottage in the country, a bungalow by the sea, a villa in Spain, or to live near your children in this country or abroad, this chapter takes a realistic view of the options and how a move can affect you emotionally. We will also look at making your home right for retirement if you decide to stay put and how to feel good about whatever decisions you come to.

Someone once said 'dreams are what life is made of', and in many ways this is true. One dream many people have, especially if they live in high-rise blocks or big towns, is to move to that dream home in the country or by the sea. For some, this dream comes true but sadly for others it is not to be.

A cottage with roses growing around the door, the sort you see on birthday cards, may seem the ideal place if you can find it to retire to. The same goes for that whitewashed coastguard's cottage or Dunroamin bungalow by the sea. If you want to move when you retire you really need to plan this, possibly a couple of years before. Ask yourself if your reasons for moving are the right ones. Have you got a rosy picture of yourself and your partner sitting day after day in sun-soaked gardens, sipping tea or wine and being happy ever after? If so, think again, be realistic, it won't be like that all the year round.

Weighing up the pros and cons

If you move it has to be because there are more practical and emotional benefits than staying where you are. Make a list rather like the following one that Ann and Bill did before they moved to the country.

Advantages of moving

1. Living in fourth-floor flat at present, stairs and lift could be a problem.
2. Bill has asthma which is aggravated by city traffic fumes.
3. Bungalow in flat location and by the sea would be ideal.
4. We would have a garden for the first time in our life.
5. We can have the dog we have always wanted.
6. Ann can get a transfer within the supermarket group that she works for so she won't lose her job.
7. Bill had an affair last year, Ann wants to make a fresh start somewhere else.

Disadvantages of moving

1. Shops are some distance away and we will need a car to get there.
2. Ann has had cancer and will have to change hospitals or travel back to where we are living now. She feels confident with the doctor she has at present and is worried about this. She is worried that if the cancer returns the treatment might not be so good where we move to.
3. We will both miss our children and grandchildren who live nearby.
4. We have no friends or relatives by the coast, which is a worry when one of us is left on our own.
5. Maintenance will be higher on a bungalow than on the flat where we are at the moment.
6. Both of us have one parent living and won't be able to keep an eye on them.

Before reading any further, make up your mind, based on Ann and Bill's list, as to whether you should move or not.

Welcome back with your list! There are always advantages and disadvantages linked with any move. All of the above are valid except the advantage of moving because of Bill's affair. Ann is saying it is so that they can make a fresh start, but although partly true she should own up to wanting to put as much space as she can between Bill and the other woman. She is probably worried that it will start again if they don't move. They need to look at why he had an affair in the first place and consider whether it could happen again with someone else.

Ann and Bill did move. They got their dog but they have not been happy. Bill hasn't settled and Ann brings up the business of the affair all the time. She is convinced Bill is still in contact with the other woman and arguments arose when he wanted to go back to see his mother when Ann was at work. The problem is not the bungalow or the area, it is the affair which is very much with them. Ann has learnt that you can't run away.

A change of scene?

Lester and Val decided they wanted to live by the sea five years ago. Unable to sell up until they retired, they got a bank loan and bought a second-hand caravan in the village where they wanted eventually to live. From March to October, for five years, they spent every possible moment there, getting to know the area, the facilities and many people. By the time they retired they were feeling like locals. They moved and have never regretted it.

A lot of people make their choice for retirement after spending a couple of holidays in a resort. What they don't realize is that once the holidaymakers have gone the town is a completely different kettle of fish. Visit your chosen spot at different times of the year, especially on wet, cold, windy days. Remember, you may not always have a car and if the shops are too far away you could face difficulties as you get older, which could lead to a feeling of isolation and possibly depression. Public transport, although abundant in the summer, may diminish during the winter months and could add to your problem. Also, some small shops which are open and well stocked for self-catering holidaymakers, may be closed or have low stocks at other times.

A few other disadvantages to moving to a popular seaside resort are over-stretched medical and health care resources and an imbalance in the age-range of the community. Young people and couples desert these seaside resorts purely because there are so many elderly people. Companies don't find it viable to move and invest there, so there are few jobs, forcing younger people to leave. Just because you turn 65 doesn't mean you want to be surrounded only by people of your age and older. Often quite the reverse. People like to see children and young couples around. If a community is made up entirely of any one age group, not just older people, it can be unhealthy.

'You have to live here for 20 years before you are accepted', one reader wrote to me about her move to a country village. Fortunately she is not one to be put off and so she ignored this and quietly got on with her life. Although no one has actually said anything to her, she thinks they are now accepting her because recently she was included in a conversation at the Post Office about some 'townies' who were buying one of the cottages. She is in her tenth year in the village.

If you have been unhappy where you are living, could a change do you good? Well, it depends on what the problem is. If the problem is external, for instance you live in a noisy or violent area, you don't get on with the neighbours, or you have never liked the area or the house, then a change would be a good idea. Far better to take the stresses away and make a new beginning somewhere else. If the problems are personal, emotional and sexual ones then moving is unlikely to make any difference, in fact it could exacerbate them. It would be better to sort out your problems, possibly with counselling, first.

If a villa in Spain appeals to you, once again think very carefully before you sell up and move. If possible, get a short let on your house here and go and rent a place in Spain to be sure you like it. A fortnight's holiday is one thing, living permanently somewhere is another, a different culture and a different way of life. A good compromise is to spend a winter in Spain and the summer months here. Life could make you feel very insecure if you jumped in at the deep end without giving it a lot of thought.

Nearer the children?

Moving to be near your children is a good idea if everyone is in agreement. If it entails emigrating then once again take a long holiday first before you give up your house here. If your family live in this country, then it could be a good idea to move near them. But remember nothing is carved in stone and there might come a time when, for one reason or another, they up sticks and move elsewhere, and you need to be aware that this could happen.

Mavis and Tim moved soon after their retirement to live near their son. Mavis was a bit dubious about the whole thing because she had never got on very well with her daughter-in-law. They chose a small house rather than a bungalow because Tim has a thing about going upstairs to bed. Mavis made up her mind that they would be as unobtrusive as they could be in the childrens' lives. Often she would turn down invitations for lunch for this very reason. This didn't deter her son and his wife, and they continued to invite them regularly. One day the son told Mavis how disappointed they were that they saw so little of them. Mavis, taken by surprise, said she thought she might be in his wife's way. Her son told her it was quite the contrary, her daughter-in-law admired her very much. For Mavis and Tim the decision to move near their son and daughter-in-law has worked out very well.

It was a different tale for Mr F. Already a widower, on retirement he sold up his house, combined the money with his son and daughter-in-law who bought a large house with a tiny annexe for him. Despite having put more than half the money towards the property, Mr F. soon found himself living in a bedsitting room with a kitchenette at one end behind louvre doors, and a shower room and toilet. When he complained he needed a separate living room, his daughter-in-law said it would be more for him to clean. His son promised to discuss it but never did. He spent a miserable two years in the annexe. He wasn't allowed into the rest of the house and was not allowed to sit in the garden when they had friends visiting. He quickly became very withdrawn and depressed.

Then he had a stroke and was rushed into hospital. On the day he

56

was to be discharged he became aware that something was wrong. Eventually the doctor said he would have to stay in one more day whilst arrangements were made for him. It turned out that the daughter-in-law had refused to have him back at the house in case he became ill again and needed looking after. She had been trying to find a home for him to go into but had failed as she had expected the Council to provide a place for him and this couldn't be done. The son took his wife's side for the sake of peace and quiet. Mr F. contacted his daughter, who immediately came down to see her father, a huge family row broke out, but the son and daughter-in-law refused to change their minds. Mr F. went to live with his daughter. He is happy there, she finds him no trouble, and he babysits for her and does as many jobs as he can. The son and daughter-in-law are still at the house, refusing to sell and give dad back his share. The whole matter is in the hands of the solicitors. Mr F. feels he was used to get them a house they otherwise could never have afforded – a costly mistake.

Helen, on the other hand, moved in with her sister on retirement, both single and never married. They have settled into a comfortable existence together, they argue occasionally but this is usually over where they should go on outings.

Somewhere smaller

Some people will want to stay put when they retire but some will want to move into a smaller or what they consider to be a more convenient home. Moving into something smaller will have some disadvantages, but most people find the advantages far outweigh these.

You will probably need to get rid of some of your furniture to avoid looking as if you are living in Steptoe's backyard. Coming to agreement over what stays and goes may cause some arguments but most couples manage this without coming to blows. Nice pieces of furniture and the odd antique going spare will probably be welcomed with open arms into your children's homes, but don't get upset if they can't see the value of that ottoman Aunt Eleanor left you, or don't want to give house room to all your spare beds.

A smaller house will mean less maintenance, less cleaning and hopefully smaller bills. It will also mean less washing because there will be fewer curtains and beds. It will also be more manageable when it comes to painting the outside, and if the garden is paved or is smaller this will reduce the work as well. People who have lived in very large houses should be careful to find something with good-sized rooms and maybe an extra room in addition to what they need, otherwise they could find themselves feeling very hemmed in and this could cause stress. Remember, if you and your partner are at home together most of the time you will need room to avoid getting in each other's way and getting on each other's nerves.

One final point on moving to a smaller house is that it may release some capital which you could use for holidays, outings, etc., to make your life more enjoyable.

Lodger in the spare room?

Taking a lodger or letting rooms in your house can be the answer to both loneliness and money problems, but do take care because many people find it turns out to be a nightmare, with lengthy legal battles to get the house back. Many years ago an elderly neighbour of mine had to go into hospital. A few days prior to this, her best friend, whom she had lived with for 50 years, died. Whilst distressed at the funeral she agreed to let the daughter and her husband, whose parents belonged to the same religious organization, rent the house during her absence. There was no written agreement and against my and others' advice she let them move into her beautiful furnished cottage on the day she went into hospital. After three weeks she went to a convalescent home and there she stayed for many months, desperately trying to get the young couple out of her home. They failed to pay rent, they moved some of her furniture into the garden shed, and the rest they used and abused. The parents would do nothing, the religious organization were at a loss to know what to do, and she had no relatives to help. Each week I would speak to her and assure her I would do everything in my power to get her home back. Eventually, with legal help we did, but she never fully recovered from the upset and worry. Sadly some months later she died. All her life she had had a strong faith in God and in trusting people. I have never forgotten Edith, her warmth, her love and her strength, what a tragedy her last few months were made so dreadful. A sad story, but one I hope you will bear in mind even if you are tempted to let anyone move into your house in your absence.

Stay safe

Do remember that although you might be pretty sprightly when you retire, you should consider that this might not always be the case as you get older, and your home should reflect this. Thinking about this might make you go through a whole range of emotions: you may feel sad, panicky or depressed. It might even be the first time you have stopped to consider becoming old and possibly ill or disabled. If this is the case, take a deep breath and tell yourself you are imagining the worst scenario. The chances are it won't come to that, but if it does, at least you are being sensible and prepared. Almost half the fatal accidents that occur in the UK happen in the home. Therefore it is especially important that your home is safe and that you have peace of mind over this.

A lot of people refurbish their home with cash sums that they receive when they retire. This is a very good time to consider the safety aspects. Polished floors and rugs may look very nice but fitted carpets are much safer and will keep your home warmer. Threadbare carpets, especially on stairs, are a big danger and if there is any money going spare then spend it on this first. If your house is old and the electrical wiring faulty it would be unwise to leave this unattended, even if it means you can't have that new three-piece suite or curtains. Don't forget to have a fire extinguisher near your kitchen and smoke alarms on each floor.

Money spent when you retire on making your home safe, comfortable and secure will be money well spent, it will stop you having nagging worries in the years to come. As an Agony Aunt I receive lots of letters from people in their seventies and eighties who are worried because jobs that have been left undone have led to a marked deterioration of their homes. This has led to real worries and stress. Get your home in good order either before or soon after you retire whilst you have the money and the energy to do it.

Different ideas?

At the end of the day you may not be able to live where you want to or have the house or bungalow that you dreamed of. This may be a disappointment but home is where you can close the door on the world and be yourself. If you are lucky enough to have a partner you love then home is where you are together.

We haven't looked yet at couples who have different ideas about where they want to live after retirement and this can lead to arguments, sulks and long silences as May and Rob found out.

May had lived in London all her life. Born and bred in the East End, she loved the hustle and bustle and had worked on a family market stall, selling fruit and vegetables and pack-filled food, for nearly 40 years. She met Rob when he had been stationed over here during the war. He is a Canadian. He came back after the war, married May and settled in their family home with her mum and dad. This is where they have stayed ever since.

May knew that Rob had always talked about going back to Canada when he retired, but she didn't take him seriously. They had never even been there for a holiday, so it came as a bit of a shock when a year before he retired he started talking about making plans. He had their house valued, wrote to house agents in Toronto, his old town, and talked about selling their business (the stall). Ignore it and he will forget about it, thought May. But he didn't, he became more persistent and excited at the prospect. May realized he was serious and so dug her heels in. He said she was selfish, he had given 50 years to live in England and wanted to go home. May said it was too much to ask of her, she needed her family and friends around her.

With all that followed they sought help from Relate. A compromise was worked out that they would go out for an extended holiday before making any decision. They did this. May could have enjoyed the holiday, but she was so adamant she wasn't going to give Canada a chance that it spoilt their stay and did little to patch things up between them. On their return, Rob said if she wouldn't go with him he would go alone. He made all the plans, even getting an apartment out there. May was dreadfully upset and started suffering with her nerves. She became agoraphobic and at the last minute Rob reluctantly stayed. Things were never really the same again after this. May gradually got over the agoraphobia and tried to make things up with Rob. She offered to go on holiday again when she felt well enough, Rob refused to even talk about it. He is pleasant to May but she feels there is always an undercurrent between them. She wants them to seek counselling again but he has refused. They still live in the family house in the East End of London and May works the stall on Friday and Saturday each week. Rob wouldn't help to begin with, but gradually he has started to. May thinks there is a glimmer of hope that they will be able to sort out what is a major disappointment for Rob and what, to May, seems an insurmountable sacrifice that she is being asked to make.

If you both have your own idea of what makes you happy when it comes to a home, if you are unhappy with what you have, it can lead to anger which is often suppressed or directed at someone who doesn't deserve it, usually your partner. It is not easy to accept what makes you discontented, but look at the alternatives: being overtaken by unhappy feelings, making those around you miserable, and then receiving back anger and hurt from them because they feel guilty that they can't change things for you.

Postbag

Q.1 My wife has always wanted to move down to the coast when we retire. Now with only six months to go she is busy getting details of houses from agents in coastal resorts across the South. She is telling everyone that we are to move, but the problem is, Vicky, I don't want to. I prefer to stay in the house where we have always lived, I don't like the idea of pulling up our roots and moving away at our time of life. The problem is I don't know how to tell her I have no intention of moving. Can you tell me how to go about this without upsetting her too much? She retired nearly three years ago from a part-time job and has been at home ever since. We own our house and we both have pensions.

I think you are being very unfair to your wife. If you don't want to move, and never have, why have you been so unkind as to let her go on thinking that you would? Also ask yourself why you are so much against the idea. Are you frightened of change or do you just like your own way all the time? Retirement can be one of two things: a time to look at your life and do many of the things you have never had time or the opportunity to do when you were working; or a time just to give up, sit around and let the rest of your life pass you by. There are hundreds of things you can do when you are retired, many of them cost very little or nothing – walking, joining an organization, doing voluntary work, going swimming, getting involved in local politics, to suggest a few of these. It is not always a good idea to move away when you retire, but for some people it is a dream come true. You must talk to your wife about this without delay. Tell her how you feel without giving her a definite decision. Your retirement together is a joint thing and it would be wrong to expect either of you to have it all your own way. You must reach some compromises otherwise your wife might just decide her retirement is not going to include you.

Q.2 We moved to the coast when we retired seven years ago. My husband John and I have never been so happy. Then he became ill and was taken into hospital with a stroke. The neighbours were very kind and offered lifts as I couldn't drive. We have made lots of friends since joining a bowling club, so even though my daughter and family are not close I had lots of support. John has been home from hospital for ten months, he is making slow progress and we are getting our life together again. My daughter wants us to move back to be near her again but it isn't what we want. We love her and her lovely husband and family but if we move back it would mean leaving a lovely home in beautiful surroundings and the many friends we have made. I look at it like this. When one of us dies the other will still have these friends. My daughter says surely family counts for more. What do you think, Vicky?

I can understand how you feel and I would say go along with these feelings. It isn't a case of who is most important, it is about what is best long term. If you had very few friends then moving to be close to your daughter might be a good option, but where you are at the moment you have lots of friends, kindness and support, so why give it up? Assure your daughter that you love her and that it is good to know that she cares so much.

Q.3 I have the opportunity to go into a sheltered accommodation flat following the death of my dear sister whom I always lived with. I accept I need someone to keep an eye on me but I am reluctant to give up my independence as I am 74.

You won't be giving up your independence, that is the whole point of sheltered accommodation. You will have your own flat where you can be alone as much as you like and do your own thing. The advantage to you of sheltered accommodation will be that help will always be at hand if and when you need it. The Warden also lives in the complex and each flat has an emergency bell system. If you are unwell or need help you just ring the bell; other than this, the Warden might pop by once a day to see if you are all right. If you feel like mixing there is usually a room where residents can meet for various kinds of social activities or just a chat. If residents prefer to stay in their own flat and not socialize then that is up to them. So you see you really do get the best of both worlds.

Accepting that you can't always have what you want is a big hurdle, but if you can do it you will find that the disappointment of being unable to have that dream cottage is not as important as you thought it was. Ask yourself, would you have been any happier if you had had it? Probably not. Happiness comes from within yourself and if you love each other it is being together that counts.

7
Happy families?

Retirement gives you more time to spend with your family if that is what you want. Not everyone feels the same, so there is no need to feel guilty if you don't want to spend extra time with yours.

Time enjoyed with children and grandchildren is time well spent. Seeing them because you feel you ought to is giving poor quality time, and unfair to all of you. You should be free to do as you please, this is your time. You have brought up your family, now take care of yourself. Do whatever makes you happy. Of course you will want to do favours for your family, but don't be bulldozed into doing things that you don't want to do just because to others you may appear 'available'.

I received a letter from a woman called Greta who had been widowed about two years before she retired. She had her own plans for her retirement which included visiting friends in South Africa and her cousin in the South of France. She planned to spend at least three months with each during the first year of her retirement. Unbeknown to Greta her daughter had her own plans for her mother. Having always wanted to teach, she applied for a last-minute place at teacher-training college to coincide with her mother's retirement in September. She had twin girls of two-and-a-half years of age and just assumed her mother would take on the job of looking after the children whilst she was at college. When confronted with the proposal only days before her retirement, Greta didn't know what to do. Having brought up four children and nursed both parents and her late husband through long illnesses she felt she needed some freedom, and the last thing she wanted was to be bogged down with children, even though they were her grandchildren and she loved them very much. She told me she felt guilty for not wanting to look after them, and her daughter's reaction had been disbelief, anger and disgust that a grandmother could refuse to help in this way. She even told Greta she had her best interests at heart when deciding on the course as Greta would need something to fill her time.

Fortunately, Greta stood her ground and wasn't pushed into doing something she didn't want to do. Babysitting she didn't mind, but becoming a full-time child-minder was a different matter. She was also angry that her daughter could take her for granted and try to arrange her life for her. Greta went abroad and her daughter made arrangements with her mother-in-law to look after the children. The relationship between them is very strained; Greta has decided that she has to take charge of her own life but hopes one day things will get back on to a better footing with her daughter.

Eva wasn't as strong as Greta and when she sold up and moved to Canada when she retired she found herself reluctantly looking after a six-month-old baby, a toddler and a dog. She had planned to stay with her daughter for just a few weeks whilst she found a flat and a job, but she couldn't do either because her daughter had given up on her child-minder expecting mum to do it instead. Many unhappy phone calls came back to friends in England, but Eva couldn't stand up to her daughter and say no. The new start she had looked forward to turned into misery, she had no car even to get out and about in and her daughter charged her the equivalent of £30 per week for her food, so her savings were being eroded as well.

Seeing your family

Family loyalty is very important especially in times of trouble but it crosses the border into the realms of 'being used' in both of these cases. Each woman reacted in a different way. How would you have reacted? Put yourself in each of these situations and be honest about what you would do. Don't let guilt get in the way. Some people will feel they would want to dedicate every second to their children and their grandchildren and that's lovely, but if, faced with a similar situation to Greta's and Eva's, you felt you couldn't go down that path then you would have to be honest with your family and say how you felt. There are, on the other hand, a lot of retired people who would desperately like to see more of their families than they do. Many retired couples would like to make frequent visits or have their family come to stay but are fobbed off with excuses, such as 'we're far too busy, the children have swimming on Saturday mornings, tuition on Sunday and the house is a shambles because we've got decorators in'. They may all be good excuses but they still hurt. What they don't realize is that the grandparents would give anything to watch little Matthew swim his first width or help Jessica with her spelling, and they wouldn't give a jot that the house wasn't tidy. They just want to see their loved ones more often. When a divorce has separated the grandchildren from their grandparents it can be even more upsetting, and this is becoming very common.

Richard and Ann never see their grandchildren. Their daughter-in-law has made certain of that. Their son has always had a behaviour problem and he became very abusive and violent with his wife. When the marriage broke up she took the children into a refuge and later disappeared with them. Their son doesn't want to see the children, his wife refused maintenance from him and he doesn't know where they are. Richard and Ann miss the grandchildren terribly and they are taking legal advice on how to get to see them.

You can't force your children or grandchildren to see you but you can make sure you keep the channels of communication open from your side. Keep in touch by letter or phone, say how much you miss them, without putting any pressure on them to visit or have you over. If you do this there is more chance of them wanting to find time to see you. Try to think back to when your children were young, all the pressures you were surrounded with, all the calls on your time. Bringing up children takes 24 hours a day, seven days a week, 52 weeks a year. It may genuinely be difficult for them to find time to see you. Being understanding may not increase your chances of seeing them more often in the short term but it should in the long term.

There are all kinds of emotions surrounding contact with children and grandchildren. It is painful to have to accept that they cannot find time for you, and it can be made much worse when you see friends with families that seem to live in each other's pockets. They usually lose no time in telling others what a close-knit family they are, which is true but it makes you hurt even more inside because you don't have this closeness with your family. You may feel that there must be something wrong with you if your family don't want you, add to this the embarrassment of other people knowing, and you can begin to feel a failure.

It is important that you don't keep all the guilt, regrets and fault at your own doorstep. Tell yourself that you are not one who is making the rift in the family and then stay positive that things may change.

When families are needed

For the very elderly, sick and housebound, visits from family are even more important. They often rely on these visits and if the visits cease altogether they are left feeling unwanted and very lonely. There are some elderly people who never see anyone from one day to the next. They cope as best they can but times like Christmas can be quite an ordeal. Some elderly people close their doors on Christmas Eve and don't see or hear from a soul until they go to the shops in the New Year, some don't even receive a Christmas card. One woman I heard from told me how she sent herself cards because nobody remembered her at Christmas or on her birthday. It is very hard to be positive under these circumstances but the stories of Millie and Bert may give some ray of hope.

Millie is disabled and confined to a wheelchair. Her family consists of one brother who lives too far away to visit, but he phones once a month, and a daughter. The daughter hasn't been near Millie since she remarried 19 years ago. Her first marriage ended in divorce. Having given up on ever seeing her daughter again Millie wrote to her local newspaper one Christmas asking if there was a family who hadn't got a 'Gran' but who would like one. A family replied to her request. The children, then aged 9, 7 and 4, had no grandparents and dearly wanted a grandma like their friends had. Millie fitted the bill. She spent Christmas Day with them, which was a great success, so much so she was invited back to see the New Year in with them. Millie is now a firm favourite with the family; they visit her, she babysits, they invite her back and take her on trips.

Bert's story is different, he liked his own company but missed corresponding with friends who had died. By chance he heard about a pen-friend club and wrote off for details. He now has pen-friends all over this country and abroad. He fills his time writing letters and waits eagerly for the post to arrive each day. He has met up with two of his pen-friends and hopes to see one from Australia when he comes to the United Kingdom to see his family.

Christmas

Going back to Christmas, this is a time when many family upsets occur, mainly over where Christmas is to be spent and who it is to be spent with. There appear to be three main trends of thought over this once people have retired. These are:

1. 'We want to stay in our own home now that we are retired and the family should make the effort and come to us.'
2. 'We've done our stint of entertaining, now we want to be invited by our children to their homes.'
3. 'We want to go away for Christmas and get away from it all.'

Each of these is perfectly normal and you may change your mind from one Christmas to another as to which suits you. That's fine so long as you don't expect everyone automatically to fit in with what you want. Your family might welcome the chance to come to you for Christmas, but don't get upset if they say they want to stay put and that you can go to them. Hopefully your children will invite you at Christmas if this is what you want, but remember they have in-laws, children who may have families, and friends that they may want to see. Have other ideas in mind if you can, just in case Christmas doesn't quite work out as you planned.

It may come as a bit of a surprise or a shock to your family if you take off on holiday at Christmas. You may have been the hub of the festivities for many years and without you around they may feel lost. Don't let this put you off. If Christmas in a country hotel appeals, or the lure of the Caribbean is too much to resist, then go! There is always next Christmas when you can drag out the Christmas tree from the loft and mend those lights for the umpteenth time.

Family troubles

Very few have avoided some family problems over the years. Perhaps it is because you are bonded together as a family that the problems which arise are often difficult to solve. People are afraid to speak their minds for fear of upsetting other family members. This is particularly true of adult children and parents. The role of parent/child is still there, whatever the age, and the commandment 'Honour thy father and mother' still holds a lot of meaning for many. Some adult children cannot express how they feel when they are angry because they fear reprimand and even punishment, which can often take the form of emotional blackmail from their parents. The elderly parents, on the other hand, may expect to rule the children's lives and those of their grandchildren, and this isn't right. Neither of these is heathly. At some time the parent and child role has to be assessed; not abandoned, just renegotiated so that each can respect the other. If you are lucky and have a really close relationship with your children please cherish and nurture it because this will be one of the most precious things that you will ever possess.

With people retiring much earlier it is not uncommon to find you are in the child/parent/grandparent roles at the same time.

Mary and Steve fall into this category. At 60 they are both retired with children in their thirties, grandchildren, and two sets of parents in their eighties who are very demanding of their time. Mary told me that their parents are totally selfish, ignoring completely the other roles that they have to fulfil. Mary's mother and father expected to visit them every Sunday morning, and Steve's parents expected to be taken shopping on Saturdays. This takes up most of the weekend which is a time they could well use to see the children who work all week. They end up snatching an hour or so together on Sunday evenings when both Mary and Steve feel shattered. What they should do is change the routine so that they see their children and take away some of the stress. Both elderly sets of parents are at home all week, so they could shop or have visitors on a weekday. This would leave the weekends free for Mary and Steve to see their children and for them to be doing what they want rather than what others decide for them. Steve's parents say they wouldn't be able to get used to shopping on any day other than Saturday, but faced with the prospect of an empty fridge I guess they could make the adjustment. Mary's parents just like to dictate to her and she needs to stand up to this for a change.

Going on holiday with your family after retirement can go one of two ways: either you will love every minute of it and revel in their company, or you may find it rather exhausting. There is a simple way of being able to go away together and avoid having problems. If you accept that your party is made up of individuals of varying ages with different needs you will understand that it might be best to have 'separate days' and 'together evenings'. You may enjoy visiting castles and places of interest, whilst the prospect of sitting on the beach all day would drive you mad. Your family on the other hand may see tramping around looking at old buildings tiring and even boring, but would welcome the opportunity to do nothing other than bask in the sun. Do your own thing during the day and meet up for an evening meal and you can't fail to have a nice time. Your children may also welcome a day on their own whilst you hold the fort with the grandchildren on the beach. It's called 'give and take' and it's what families should be all about!

Postbag

Q.1 My son and his wife have taken it for granted that I would look after their three-month-old baby whilst they go on holiday. I know Penny needs a rest but I don't think it is a good idea to stop breast feeding and put him on a bottle so that they can go away. Also I am worried I won't be able to cope with the broken nights. I am 69 and I need my sleep, I don't want to disappoint them but I don't feel happy about it.
Then tell them . . . you want to postpone the holiday until your grandson

is sleeping through the night, is on solids and not dependent on breast-feeding. To go on holiday, change him on to a bottle and at the same time leave him with someone else will certainly unsettle him. He will miss his mum, and sometimes it takes a while for a baby to accept a bottle instead of the breast. Offer to babysit as a compromise so that they can get out occasionally and say you will gladly look after him when he is a bit older.

Q.2 We have done so much for our son and his wife. We gave them the money for a deposit for a flat when they got married six months ago out of a lump sum my husband got on his retirement. We decorated it whilst they were on honeymoon and gave them some really nice pieces of furniture. In return they hardly ever invited us to visit and when I called round to see my daughter-in-law on the off-chance she didn't even open the door, although her car was outside and she was obviously in. What have we done wrong? My son and his wife are in their mid thirties.

Can you remember how you felt when you got your first home? You probably wanted to shut the door on the world and just be together. Well this is how they feel. You have done a lot for them now they need to put their own mark on their flat. Try to understand and very soon things will change.

Q.3 The only time my daughter gets in touch with me is when she needs money. I haven't got much savings left at 72 but she seems intent on taking all I have. Divorced twice, she is out of work and won't look for a job and lives on social security. She makes me feel like a heel if I don't give her what she wants. She is my only family so I suppose I can't complain.

That doesn't make it right! Tell her there is no more money for her and mean it. You can't leave yourself with nothing and you are not doing her any favours by encouraging her to remain out of work.

Whatever your family problems may be, with love, understanding and a bit of give and take, hopefully you will be able to sort them out. Never lose sight of the fact that other people may walk away if you upset them, but your family will usually stick by you through thick and thin. They are the greatest gift you will ever have in your life.

8
Keep fit, stay healthy

Probably only a small minority of people reach retirement in the peak of physical and mental fitness. Many more arrive rather overweight, slightly out of breath, and when it comes to running to catch a bus they would rather wait for the next one to arrive. As for mental fitness, working for 40 or so years, bringing up a family, trying to make the money stretch, going from the high spots in life to the low ones, dealing with fate, with surprises and major disappointments . . . is it any wonder that many people feel anything but mentally fit?

Well, that can change, along with your physical fitness, because now you are going to have time to look after your body. By looking after your body, I don't mean becoming sedentary, settling down in that chair in front of the television so that you don't wear yourself out. I mean improvement. Whatever your state at the moment, even if you suffer with arthritis or any other condition, you can take charge of yourself, your mind and your body. Remember those sayings so often used: 'mind over matter', 'positive thinking', 'inner healing'. I firmly believe that good health comes from within, whatever we feel affects the way we behave and the way our bodies work. When something goes wrong in your life and you are sad and unhappy, think of the way it affects you. You can feel tired and unmotivated, get headaches, mouth ulcers, upset stomach, pains, tingling limbs, diarrhoea, spots and styes. The unhappiness you feel inside sends signals all over the body and is reflected in physical symptoms.

Likewise, good news, happy events and a contentment with life makes you feel good and affects the way your body behaves. How many times have you seen someone, who seems to have so many things wrong with them that they have been labelled hypochondriac, suddenly change, if only for a short time, when something good comes into their life? This chapter is about health and fitness and about gaining this, not only through exercise and good diet but also through learning to relax and getting the balance of emotions right. If you do this you will have a feeling of well-being right through your body which will help you to become mentally and physically fit and stay that way for as long as possible.

So where shall we start? No, you can stop worrying and put off that trip to buy the shorts and sports equipment . . . we will talk about that later, when you are feeling ready for it. It makes sense to have a complete MOT at your doctor's and get a clean bill of health at the start of your retirement.

The 'one-mile test'

Let me first introduce you to the 'one-mile test'.

I want you to find a good one-mile circular walk as flat as possible. Make sure you have comfortable shoes or trainers. Before, or soon after, you retire I want you to walk this mile at a comfortable pace and time how long it takes you. Also, make a note of how you feel at the end of it. If you have had a heart condition or high blood pressure, please consult your doctor before you do this. This one-mile test is going to be the yardstick that will tell you how fit you are as you progress through retirement.

Once a year (minimum), on the anniversary of your first walk, I want you to repeat the walk. By the time you take and the way you feel, you will be able to judge for yourself whether you are keeping fit or letting yourself go. Providing you pick a day when you are feeling in reasonably good health, this should be a good pointer. Don't force yourself to do it if you are not well and *stop* if you find it too much. If you feel the same or better, then you are doing all right; if you take much longer and feel worn out at the end of it then you should ask yourself if you are letting yourself go and whether a check-up is in order. You may want to do this more often as part of your fitness programme; this is fine.

Get yourself a small notebook and mark it 'The one-mile retirement test'. Not only will it keep a fitness record for you, it will also give you an incentive to keep fit.

Whilst walking this mile I want you to use this time to relax mentally as well. Breathe steadily as you walk and imagine each breath that you take in is the 'breath of life', that it is washing away all those aches and pains and worries. If the sun is shining, imagine that the warmth from it is a healing light that bathes the body and mind. If there is a wind or breeze, imagine this is blowing away all your tensions and stress. I walk by the sea several times a week and as I breathe in the sea air I imagine this is running through my body and cleansing it of any rogue cancer cells that might be there (I had cancer in my neck some years ago). I have been practising this kind of technique for over five years now and I think it has helped keep me in the best of health. It can do the same for you.

71

Keep fit, have fun

The one-mile test will give you a good indication of whether you are keeping fit or not, but a good walk every day will keep you agile and mentally alert throughout the year. Probably one of the best types of exercise you can take up is swimming, because it combines the three Ss – Stamina, Strength and Suppleness. I would like to see all senior citizens heading for the pools if their health allows them.

Can't swim? You are never too old to learn. There is a woman who lives close to me who learnt to swim when she was over 80. Now 85, she lives with her husband in a bungalow on the beach and swims every day in the sea. Lots of you will say 'I will look terrible in a swimming costume'. Take a look around any pool, very few look like models, most come in a variety of shapes and sizes. Who cares and who notices – no one. It is your self-conscious feelings that are getting in the way. Cycling, tennis, golf, squash, bowls, badminton and rambling are all sports that retired people can enjoy.

So is dancing. Thousands of people all over the country go dancing every week. Whether it is sequence, old time, modern, barn dance or country and western, it is a way of keeping fit. Dancing also offers you the opportunity to make friends and above all enjoy yourself, and this is very important to keep yourself in the right emotional state.

As a tap-dancer of sorts myself I can vouch for the fun and fitness tap-dancing can bring. My group has men and women from 14 to late seventies. As we dance to 'Hooray for Hollywood' anyone watching would be hard put not to smile or even laugh. Our dance line is seldom straight, we keep in time with each other as much as we can, and the concentration on our faces as we dance would have to be seen to be believed. When we go wrong we laugh so much that the tears run down our faces. So why not give it a try?

Playing bowls is fast becoming one of the most popular sports for the retired, and no wonder. What better way to get exercise, make friends and keep mentally alert? If you play for a team, you also get to visit lots of places when your team plays away. Being part of a team, and achieving together, gives you a wonderful sense of belonging and purpose.

Some will take up step, aerobics, tennis, badminton, golf or squash. All are an ideal way of keeping fit, with the bonus of keeping your co-ordination sharp and your mind alert.

By now there will be those of you who feel like throwing this book out of the window. But if you hate the water, and the thought of getting undressed and getting your hair wet every time you go swimming fills you with dread, donning a tracksuit and setting off jogging does little to inspire you, and any form of sport which involves co-ordination with a ball fills you with dread, well don't despair, there is something out there for you. Have you got a dog you can take for a leisurely walk each day? No? Well, borrow a neighbour's! I know several women who do this and one who does baby and toddler walking. She sets off with the neighbour's children for a walk in their buggies. Not only does she enjoy the walk and the childrens' company but it gives her pleasure to know she is giving some of the younger neighbours a well-earned rest from the children for an hour or so. Before this, as a widow, she had felt pretty useless and unfit. Now, having shed half a stone, she feels much fitter and emotionally happy.

If you live in a flat area, a bike is another way of keeping fit and mentally alert, so is joining a rambling club or going on projects with the British Conservation Society. Both offer physical fitness to fit in with individual needs, mental stimulation and the chance to make new friends.

Fishing, sailing, camping, water sports, orienteering – anything that gets you out of the house and into the fresh air is great for your body and your mind. Don't forget sex – that's good exercise for the body and the mind.

Your diet

Keeping the body fit with exercise is good, but you have to look at your body as a whole, and that includes your mind, your emotions and what you eat – they are all very closely linked. If you likened it to a car, it is no good looking after only part of it; to get the most from it you have to make sure every bit is in the best possible working order. It is the same with your body.

Feel unfit in your body, and you will lose your appetite and worry. If you don't eat properly you will feel lethargic, forgetful and run down. If your mind is in a turmoil, you can't relax, physical symptoms will appear and you will feel less inclined to eat properly.

So let's look at your diet. As you get older, dietary requirements alter but it is still important to eat a healthy balanced diet. It is also important to keep an interest in food so that you enjoy cooking and eating. Often problems with disability, getting to the shops in bad weather, or with teeth and denture problems can lead to loss of interest in food, so it is important to have the right mental approach. Make sure you enjoy what you eat.

Many older people say 'We don't need much at our age, we are maintaining our bodies not building them', but this is not true. You need a good diet for a healthy blood, digestive and nervous systems. Eating a wide range of foods, including potatoes, pasta, rice cereals, bran, fresh vegetables, fruit, fish, meat and poultry to suit your taste, plus some dairy products, including milk, will help this. Cut down on the fats and increase the amount of oily fish you eat as tests have found they contain Omega-3 Polyunsaturates, which may help stop blood-clotting. Although it is hard, try to keep the right weight for your height and body frame; overweight people seldom feel well and it affects their joints, back and mobility. If you are underweight you may be more susceptible to coughs and colds, infections and diseases.

Fibre is important to keep regular and we all know how miserable we can be if we are not. Calcium is essential to fend off osteoporosis, and don't forget to get out of the house as much as possible, as we get a lot of our vitamin D from exposure to sunlight. If you are housebound, eat oily fish, eggs, margarine and fortified cereals at breakfast time. Step up eating fruit and vegetables, as cuts and wounds tend to heal less easily if your vitamin C levels are low. Lots of people find they are less thirsty as they get older and go without drinks for long periods. Whether you are thirsty or not, drink plenty, your body needs plenty of fluids and people who drink very little in the day often complain of headaches. Make sure a lot of your drinks are water and not just coffee and tea, too much of these are bad for you. If you are worried about the cost of food, do check you are getting all the benefits that you are entitled to.

Coping with stress

A healthy relaxed body and mind won't cost you anything except a little of your time each day. Many people fail to recognize when they are stressed, so here is an explanation of what stress is and the warning signs.

Some stress is good for everyone and we all experience it when we are anxious, excited or feeling tense. When it starts to interfere with your life and you become tense, nervous and have physical symptoms, then you have to do something about it. Here are some of the symptoms that can indicate your stress levels have risen:

- insomnia
- tiredness
- palpitations
- irritability
- anger
- crying for no reason

- loss of appetite
- aches and pains
- lack of concentration
- loss of interest in things you used to enjoy
- nausea
- sexual problems
- hyperventilation
- butterflies in the stomach
- clammy or cold hands.

See your doctor if you feel tense and experience one or more of these symptoms. There are also ways in which you can help yourself. Regular exercise helps to combat stress and makes your body and mind healthier.

Think logically and rationally about any problems you may have and don't dwell on what has happened in the past or worry about what may happen in the future. Concentrate on what is happening now, that's what is important. If you feel tense and you are having difficulties sleeping, then the following relaxation exercises will help. Do these regularly every day, first thing in the morning and when you get into bed at night and you will find they help. Always start with the relaxation of the body exercises and then go on to the relaxation of the mind ones.

Relaxation: body

1. Sit or lie comfortably.
2. Close your eyes gently. Become aware of your body and how it feels.
3. Concentrate on your breathing – slow and gentle.
4. Tighten the muscles in your feet. Be aware of how it feels. Slowly let the tension go. Let your feet feel relaxed and heavy.
5. Using this technique of tightening and relaxing, continue up the body. Tighten and relax your calf and thigh muscles. Repeat for the other leg. Then use the method on buttocks, abdomen, back, chest and shoulders; then hands, lower and upper arms, neck and face.
6. When your whole body is relaxed, become aware of your breathing again. Relax the whole body further. Lie quietly for several minutes.
7. When you are ready, slowly bring your body back to a state of readiness. Open your eyes while still lying down. Do not sit up until you are quite ready.

Relaxation: mind

1. Sit or lie comfortably.
2. Close your eyes gently.
3. Relax all your muscles from your feet to your face.

4. Breathe through your nose and listen to your breathing.
5. Repeat the word 'one' or any other sound you have chosen for this purpose. Relax further.
6. Continue for 10 to 20 minutes. Do not use an alarm. You will soon learn to judge the time naturally. At the end, let yourself become gradually aware. Sit quietly for a while before getting up.

During your relaxation time, do not try and force yourself to be relaxed. This will come naturally. Let any distracting thoughts flow through your mind rather than trying to banish them. Gently bring your word or thought back in. Most benefit is achieved by practising twice a day, but not too soon after a heavy meal.

Meditation and visualization

Let us now look at the benefits of meditation and visualization to having an emotionally stable and happy retirement. There is no doubt in my mind that these can be invaluable. Many people find yoga gives more benefit to their lives, especially in retirement when they have more time to practise and meditate. A very close friend of mine, Nerys Dee the famous dream analyst, sadly died but during her life she worked very hard in the area of self-help and healing. She used to say 'Life is not a rehearsal, it is the real thing'. I know the benefits of being positive when cancer strikes and how a positive attitude, combined with a healthy diet, relaxation and visualization can help at any time during our lives. Many people find visualization rather difficult when they start, but if you stick with it for a couple of weeks it gets easier and gradually becomes almost second nature.

Whether you feel stressed, worried, unwell or have a serious illness, visualization is for you, so let's make a start.

You need a warm comfortable room and you can either lie on a bed or sit in a comfortable chair, preferably with your feet and arms supported.

You will also need some soft and gentle background music. Settle yourself down at a time when you are reasonably sure you will not be disturbed. Go through the relaxation of the body, then the relaxation of the mind exercises, and then start your visualization.

You can imagine yourself anywhere where you feel tranquil, maybe on a warm sunny deserted beach, walking through the countryside or even in a church, whatever pleases you. Imagine the sun's rays bathing you in sunlight, sunlight that heals and calms you.

During your visualization you can visualize yourself walking peacefully around your chosen spot. Everything is perfect, from the colour and the perfume of the flowers to the breeze that makes the sun's rays feel so gentle.

After 5 or 10 minutes, start to let go of your visualization and see yourself as you are lying or sitting at home relaxed and happy. Gradually open your eyes and return to the present. Allow yourself another 5 minutes just to relax before getting up.

If you feel you need healing for a specific illness, or you are stressed, use what is called the blue pool visualization. Once again it can be anywhere you want it to be, in a garden, in the mountains, by the sea, you choose.

In this visualization you undress and walk down beautiful marble steps into the blue waters of the pool and immerse yourself. No one else is there unless you want them to be, and as the water covers your body imagine it cleanses it of all the ailments and gives you a deep inner peace.

As you leave the pool there are piles of warm white fluffy towels which you wrap around yourself. As they envelop your body the warmth flows through to complete your visualization and healing process.

You can use your imagination and invent your own visualizations. They will help to bring a sense of peace to you even when things seem bad.

Postbag

Q.1 All my life I have enjoyed sport as a participant but never really enjoyed watching it. What bothers me most as I approach retirement is that my ability to participate in sports that I love will gradually diminish. I missed football when I finally had to give it up and became quite miserable for some time. I then took up tennis, badminton, squash, and now I really love them. I would like it if my wife and I took up golf when I retire but she says we are too old to start tramping around golf courses. What do you think?

Starting with your wife's comments first, that really shows a very negative attitude towards retirement and her age. She obviously feels old and is letting this put up barriers for what she and in turn you can do. Many wives encourage their partners to take up exercise but never join in themselves, it is almost as if they think that their husbands do it for both of them. Thousands and thousands of people take up golf in retirement and what a wonderful way to get out in the fresh air, take exercise and get enjoyment. This is a definite yes for you, and I hope you can persuade your wife to give it a go too. Many people take up sport in their retirement but those like yourself who have played all their life should have no problem and be able to continue for many years to come. My husband played badminton with a club a few years ago and although he and many of the other members were in their forties some of the best players were well into their seventies and have played for years. So get out there and join them.

Q.2 A friend told me that she does yoga and meditation, she seems a very calm and peaceful person. I would like to be like her but I am always worried that if I get into a meditation I might get stuck, so to speak, and wouldn't be able to pull myself out of it. Does this seem silly?

No, it doesn't. Lots of people say the same. With meditation and any form of relaxation or visualization you are in complete control, no one is taking you over, telling you what to do or putting you into a trance that you can't get out of. Although thinking deeply, you can stop whenever you want to, but because of the very relaxed state your body goes into it is always advisable slowly to bring your thoughts back to the room where you are and sit or lie quietly for a few moments before getting up to your feet. Yoga is an excellent way to keep your body and mind fit, so why not give it a try?

Q.3 Although I have never done any physical exercise other than walking the dog, I would like to do something now I am retired. I am 64 and my wife is partially sighted. Is there anything not too difficult for beginners that we could do together?

Swimming is one of the best forms of exercise and it certainly is something you could do together. Choose a time when the pool is not too crowded. The Manager of the pool will tell you what time is best, both for beginners and for your wife. You won't want to be there when the pool is full of children and with her limited vision your wife might find it rather difficult to know where to swim to avoid children who are jumping into the pool. You might also like to go to swimming lessons, and often there are concessionary rates for those who are retired, both for use of the pool and for lessons.

Q.4 All of this keep fit lark gets on my nerves, I can't see the point of dragging myself off to the gym, packing up things that I enjoy, such as good food and drink. I don't smoke. When your time is up it's up, that's what I say, so why put yourself through misery for this, I can't see the point.

I think you can. In fact, I think it bothers you a lot, otherwise why would you be writing to me? No one expects you to do anything, it's your body and mind, treat it as you will. You may live for years but you might not be so mentally alert or agile in your seventies and eighties as others who do look after their bodies. Of course you don't know when you will die, but wouldn't it be nice to be as fit as possible and enjoy all the years ahead? You don't have to do anything other than eat sensibly and take plenty of walks to keep yourself reasonably fit. It's up to you.

A fit body will help you to enjoy your retirement more fully, but never underestimate the importance of a fit mind. Emotions are our life force, without them we would be nothing. Get the emotions in a muddle and nothing will ever seem right, get the balance correct and the possibilities for the future will be endless.

9

Relationships, romance and sex

Yes . . . sex! No, it won't harm you, you are not too old and it is not too late to be more adventurous. In this chapter we are going to look at sex, with a particular emphasis on dispelling the myth that sex is only for the young and that it is disgusting if older people indulge in it. For those of you who enjoy sex there is certainly no reason why it can't be a regular part of your life, whatever your age. If it isn't for you then maybe the section on romance may still be of interest. For those of you who feel romance has gone out of the window long ago, don't despair, this chapter will help you find it again.

Earlier in this book we looked at where your relationship was at as you approached retirement, being honest about your feelings, your worries, your disappointments and what you want from your relationship now. This chapter is going to dig deep into your innermost thoughts and hopefully clear it of any guilt, disappointment or hangups that linger there. How you react will depend on the amount of honesty you put into dealing with issues that arise. It may make you feel sad and angry with the way things are or pleasantly satisfied with what you have. It isn't for the faint hearted so let's get going.

Nourishing a relationship

Relationships are a bit like plants, if you look after them they flourish, if you don't they wither and die. What a relationship needs for it to keep alive will vary from one couple to another, also between the man and the woman. There are exceptions, but many women who reach retirement age will complain that there is no romance left in their relationship and that they are taken for granted. The men on the other hand say their wives have 'gone off' or 'lost interest' in the sexual side of the relationship, with the menopause being the top culprit for the switch-off.

If you study these two statements it is interesting to see that they are talking about different things. She, about a very emotional thing – 'romance' – and he, a physical act – 'sex'. Someone once said: 'Women are into romance, men are into lust' and it can often appear this way. Sadly many men confuse sex with being romantic. I have lost count of the number of letters I have received over the years from women who wish their partners would do something romantic, say they love them or give them a cuddle, without it always having to lead to having sex. If only men could see how much they could gain from this. Often the cuddles would lead on to sex and there would be loving and giving on both sides. What tends to happen is the woman at some point gets so fed up with the lack of affection that she loses interest, switches off and even dreads sex. What we have to do in this chapter is to find ways of entwining love, sex, affection and romance so that both men and women are happy. Neither should have it all their own way, that isn't fair.

Romance

In the search for romance we have to go right back to when a relationship began. However long ago, I doubt if anyone has forgotten the excitement of the first meeting, the longing to see each other and the way you were. Maybe you felt you were floating on cloud nine and wanted to swing round lamp posts and to tell the world how much you were in love. Whether you were 16 or 50 when you met your partner, the feeling of excitement, anticipation and love will have been the same.

You don't have to be 16 to feel like a teenager inside! Love has no age barrier! The looks, glances, smiles, laughter and tender moments were all part of it. You couldn't bear being apart . . . you were in love with this man or this woman and you didn't care who knew. So what happened to all those magic moments? Did you leave them behind or did you secretly hold them in your heart wishing they could be brought out again? Most women say they wish they could, and probably a lot of men secretly wish this too. You have to remember that although your outer body may change as it gets older, inside you probably feel the same as you always did, but worries, family and life may have cast a shadow over this.

One of the biggest things a relationship has to survive is bringing up a family. If you are a woman, ask yourself if you always put the children first and in doing so neglected your relationship with your husband. Did he come bottom in the pecking order? If a man, ask yourself if you felt jealous and resentful of the amount of time your wife or partner spent on the children and if you often felt left out. It is a sad fact that many women have been 'super mums' but pretty poor wives to their husbands because they put their relationship on hold whilst the children were being brought up, only to expect to pick it up where they left off when the children were gone. They are then hurt and upset by the fact the husband has lost interest in them, has channelled his interests into other things, perhaps even an affair.

Of course the children needed attention and looking after, but the man you set out with is the man you will hopefully end your days with. The children are only on loan for a short time, they then get on with their own lives. The resentment some men feel over what has happened can be very deep rooted and they may build a shell around themselves to protect their hurt feelings. This may be hard to crack but it isn't impossible if their partner is determined to make up for lost time. As for the man, he can stay with his hurt feelings or try to understand how easily this kind of problem can arise. Looking back he may feel angry that he provided well for the family and yet his emotional needs were always ignored and his wife was far too busy to be bothered with him. Stay with these feelings and the unhappiness will go on and on. Deal with them by telling your partner how you feel, put them firmly in the past and then you will be able to make a fresh start.

Try to remember your partner as the man or woman they were when you first met. You must do this properly, not just a fleeting glimpse into the past. It has to be a real 'delve in' exercise, like the one that follows.

To do this you will need to be alone in a warm quiet room and it would help if you could find as many photographs of when you first met as you can. If you can't find these, then your wedding photograph will be the next best. Spread these on a table in front of you.

Sit very still and comfortably in a chair at a table and breathe in slowly and deeply with your eyes closed, trying to recall as much about those first days, weeks and months together as you can. If the memories make you happy let this go into a smile, likewise if sad it won't hurt to shed tears. When you can recall no more, open your eyes slowly and let them rest on one of the photographs. Stay with that photograph, let your fingers run over it, let the memories it brings flood back over you. Look at the expression on your and your partner's faces. What do you see? Love? Happiness? Laughter? Absorb this by looking at the picture for at least a minute.

Move on through the pictures doing the same with each one. Let yourself float back in time as you soak up the feelings of the past. The point of this exercise is to get in touch with the emotions you felt when you first met, to recognize the things that made you happy to be with your partner.

Now we move on to the part you played in making them happy. Repeat the exercise, but this time, instead of thinking about what you got from those early days, concentrate on what you did to make your partner look so happy. Only when you can do this will you be able to start to put the romance back into your relationship by rekindling the spark, by doing the things you used to do.

We get out of any relationship what we put into it. At the beginning of your relationship you put in love, affection, attention and an element of excitement. Ask yourself what you put in now. How often do you say you care? Try some of the following. Instead of saying 'He doesn't care about me', try saying 'I care about you'. When you wish she would show more feeling towards you try saying 'I love you'. The three words 'I love you', a smile, a hug, a wink, the casual brush of the hand on the face or hair, holding hands, putting your arms around your partner when they are tired or upset, and a kind word each day, will change a dull, boring relationship into a romantic one again.

If you think you are past all this, think again. Some people find true love for the first time after retirement and they do all these things without a second thought. It is so easy to fall in love, but even easier to let a relationship go to waste. The love and magic is still there for most people if they look for it, but you have first to look inside yourself, find and reflect those original feelings to your partner. It will be like the blossoming of a flower. It may be slow to start but it will eventually bloom. Don't be bogged down or put off by age – it's just a number.

Yes, sex!

When it comes to sex, age is thought of as a barrier that people either stop at or hide behind. Those that stop are the ones who either have problems that they are too embarrassed to talk about, or who get bored, or who think sex is only for the young. Those that hide are the ones who have good sex lives but who worry about their age, or that it is something they should keep quiet about in case anyone thinks they are depraved, or that it will harm them. The reason for this is that sex is very much portrayed in films, on television and in the media as being for the young, so much so that teenagers often have a fit when they find out their parents are still sexually active in their forties, let alone in their seventies or eighties. 'Disgusting' is how one teenager described it to me when he came across his parents making love. Why? Because everything sexy is geared to the young. Clothes, music, magazines . . . the lot! How often do we see anything which even loosely implies that people of all ages, including those in their sixties, seventies and eighties, enjoy sex? Very seldom. Let me say now quite clearly: sex is for everyone! It's fun, it's free and it keeps you fit.

There will be those of you who will be enjoying this area of your life to the full, others who for whatever reason prefer not to indulge. Neither is right or wrong. Do what makes you happy. Difficulties only arise when there are different needs between a couple or there are specific problems.

I would like to go through a list of specific sexual problems for those who are experiencing difficulties and wish things could be different.

Let's start with one of the most common sorts of problems: boredom, lack of interest, lack of arousal and 'can't be bothered' to have intercourse. These problems are mainly experienced by women, but sometimes by men. Boredom can come about when a partner is very selfish in a relationship and doesn't take care of their partner's needs. The man who has gone through his marriage making love with the sole purpose of reaching a climax, with no thought to how his wife feels, has no one but himself to blame when she switches off from sex.

Beverley was the wife of one such man. During all her married life, sex with Malcolm would be over in a couple of minutes before she had even got aroused. She became more and more fed up with it, she tried talking to Malcolm, even asking him to carry on caressing her after he had climaxed, but Malcolm would say he was tired or he didn't feel like it. When sex became uncomfortable after the menopause, due to vaginal dryness, Beverley would not have sex any more. There were arguments, but eventually these died out and Malcolm became very resentful. Beverley wouldn't even touch him for fear it would lead to intercourse.

Some people accept whatever comes their way but others are always hopeful that things will change. For lack of interest in sex, or for any of the problems mentioned, the Masters and Johnson techniques have been successful for couples over many years. They put no pressure on either partner to have intercourse, but because they are very sensual they often lead on to it. The techniques encourage both partners to find ways of pleasing each other and are ideal to help them get back into a loving sexual relationship.

Pleasure techniques for couples

The following techniques are based on methods used by sex therapists Masters and Johnson.

You will need a warm room, massage oil (baby oil is quite suitable) and warm towels.

The aim of these techniques is to reawaken your sexual feelings and to encourage trust and communication between you and your partner. You will need to exchange information about the giving and receiving of sensual touch. You should both ask about the effectiveness of touching each other's bodies. When something feels good tell your partner and when a touch needs to be altered, because you either don't like it or it is not quite right, you should say so.

Start by sharing a warm bath and slowly soaping each other all over, but exclude the genitals. Then move from the bathroom to a warm room where you will carry out a mutual massage. You will probably find it better, as you are using oil, to spread warm towels on the bed or wherever you decide to lie. Some people find it enjoyable, especially in the winter, to lie in front of a fire (but not too close). The woman should massage the man first and then reverse this. The object of the massage is to discover each other's erogenous zones and to find out what you both enjoy. On the first occasion, the genitals should not be massaged, but the rest of the body can be. Each massage should last about 20 minutes or more. Over future sessions the warm bath and massage are repeated but then the genital areas can be included. It is important to remember that the genital area should be treated the same as the rest of your body (to find out which parts are most sensitive) and that the genitals are not being massaged in order to obtain a climax.

After a few sessions you should continue the warm bath but the massage positions change. The man leans back against pillows in a sitting position whilst the woman seats herself between his legs with her back resting against his chest. The man massages the woman as before, but in this different position. This time you need to look at different types of touch, pressure and movement, as well as sensitivity. Over a period of about eight sessions you will probably reach a stage when both of you want intercourse, whereas previously you have not. Although you may refrain from having intercourse for several sessions this does not mean you have to refrain from reaching a climax during the massage.

The idea of these techniques is to allow a couple to find out what they enjoy without the pressure of feeling that they have to have intercourse.

Impotence

For men, the most common sexual problem is impotence and it brings with it for many men a total loss of self-esteem. Because of embarrassment, most men refuse to seek help and may not even want to discuss it with their partners. This is sad because in most cases they could be helped. Isn't it strange that if we have a broken limb, a physical illness or even a mental one, we go to see our doctors, yet once it becomes anything to do with our genital area or our sexuality it is as if the shutters come down and we hide behind them? There is no shame in seeking help on any sexual problem and it is a great pity when people fail to do so. Often when a man becomes impotent he shuts off completely from his partner, leaving her feeling unloved, unwanted and as though it must be her fault. The relationship becomes cold, they grow apart, with so much left unsaid and the cause of the impotence never found or rectified.

There are many things that cause impotence and it is important to understand this. It has nothing to do with being less of a man or being past it. Amongst the causes are fatigue, temporary stress, or excessive alcohol, which can cause temporary erectile failure and which most men suffer from at some point in their lives. More long-term erectile failure can have physical causes, including circulation and nerve disorders, certain medical conditions such as diabetes, and the side-effects of some medications such as those used for controlling blood pressure. It can also have psychological causes such as depression, anxiety, worry about poor sexual performance, an unhappy marriage or unresolved sexual orientation.

Many doctors are now keeping up to date with the latest impotence research and treatment. When a patient sees their doctor it will be their attitude not their age that will determine whether they can be helped, so no one should be put off getting help for fear that they are too old. Some men will prefer to seek help on their own, others with their partner. Do what is right for you, but don't shut your partner out; talk to them about what is going on so that they are able to give you the help and support you need. Men who don't do this often avoid sexual contact altogether, making up wild and extravagant reasons for doing so. This can lead to a wife worrying there is something wrong with her or that her husband is having an affair.

So what can be done? Simple things like quitting smoking can improve the way things are. Getting medication changed through your GP may also help. In a few cases, impotence is caused by an imbalance in the hormones, and this can be adjusted. Other methods include professional counselling, injection therapy, vacuum devices, surgical treatment, and penial prostheses when all other methods have been tried. Your doctor can refer you to a specialist if he or she doesn't have the expertise in impotence, and your individual case will have to be assessed before any treatment can be tried. If your doctor says he or she can't help, don't take no for an answer, look around for a doctor who can. The good news for shy men is that there is now an Impotence Association with a helpline in London on 0181 769 7791.

For Jean and Clive the problem of impotence came about because of

Clive's loss of self-confidence. Having found out that Jean had been having an affair for two years, he rapidly lost confidence in himself. He had always been a workaholic and spent very little time with Jean. Although their sex life was good, Jean turned to someone else because he gave her the time, affection and attention she never got from Clive. The affair ended when Clive found out, and sex between them ceased for nearly a year whilst they were having counselling and sorting themselves out. When they eventually tried to make love, Clive couldn't get an erection, he was very upset. Further attempts over the coming weeks had the same result. Clive was devastated. He wouldn't discuss it with Jean but he would make snide remarks, such as 'I expect you will be finding yourself a real man'.

Clive wouldn't seek help and in the end it was Jean who talked to their doctor. He explained to Jean the problem was not just Clive's, it was a joint problem but brought on by his fears of not being good enough to satisfy her. The affair to him had been proof of this. The doctor went on to say that the problem was a psychological one that they could overcome together. It needed a lot of love from Jean over the coming months. She never made Clive feel bad about his lack of erection and she told him she really loved and needed him. They started to use the Masters and Johnson techniques, and finally one night Clive got an erection. Jean told me they nearly didn't have intercourse because they couldn't stop laughing when it happened. Then the laughter turned to tears . . . but ones of joy. After this they never looked back.

Ada and George's case was different. His impotence came on over a period of six months. He thought it was old age because he was 68, but when he wrote to me and told me he was on medication for blood pressure I advised him to go back to his doctor as this could be causing the problem. This turned out to be so. His medication was changed and the problem resolved itself.

Premature ejaculation

Premature ejaculation is mainly thought of as a problem that young people have whilst in a new relationship, but it can affect older age groups as well. Like impotency, if it happens once, especially in a new relationship, the man starts to worry that it might happen again, and because of this it usually does. This problem can often be overcome by having a period of cuddling and resting for 20 minutes after the first ejaculation and then having intercourse again. Alternatively, the woman may not mind if the man pleases her in other ways – maybe by touch or orally. The main thing is to talk about it rather than let it have an adverse affect on your relationship. If premature ejaculation proves to be a major problem in your relationship there are techniques called the 'squeeze technique' that may help, but to do these you will need a very loving and patient wife as they do take time and effort on her part. Here they are for those of you who may wish to try.

The 'squeeze technique'

When a couple are experiencing problems due to premature ejaculation, the first thing to do is to promise each other that you won't have intercourse until you can develop control. This does not mean you cannot make love or indulge in a lot of cuddling.

You will need to be either on the floor or on a bed with a firm back rest, for example a wall or a headboard. The woman sits with her back against the wall with her legs spread wide apart. The man sits with his back to her with his legs spread wide apart and parallel to his partner's. The woman then reaches round the man and takes the penis in her thumb and index finger, just above and below the ridge where the cap on top of the penis meets the shaft. She then rubs gently as if she were masturbating the man, until he almost ejaculates. It is up to the man to tell his partner when this is about to happen. At this moment, just before her partner is about to ejaculate, she should squeeze the head and the shaft of the penis really tightly for several seconds. This should stop her partner ejaculating and it will also cause some loss of erection, but this does not matter. There should be a short pause and then they should start again. If possible, this should be continued for between 30 to 45 minutes.

It takes time to get it right, but once you do you will find that you will not ejaculate once pressure is applied. This is basically what is known as a 'tease technique'. Many people worry that they will hurt their partner, but there is no truth in this. They also worry about losing some of the man's erection, but this shows that the technique is working. So long as he loses some erection each time they do it, the length of time it will take the man to get aroused will get longer between each session. This technique should be continued as regularly as possible for at least three weeks.

After three weeks you can then attempt to have intercourse. The woman should take the upper position and the man should lie on his back with a pillow under his head. Practise the 'squeeze technique' for several minutes and then the woman should gently insert the penis into the vagina very slowly and then the couple should lie still. If the man starts to lose control, the woman should quickly and gently remove herself and apply the 'squeeze technique' very hard. Don't be afraid to do this. It won't cause any harm.

Gradually, the man should find he is able to maintain his erection for longer and not suffer premature ejaculation.

Other problems

For many women, after the menopause, one of the greatest turn-offs is vaginal dryness and the discomfort it causes. Women who remain frequently sexually active have fewer problems of this kind, but for those who do there is a very simple remedy, try using one of the lubricants, such as Senselle or K Y jelly, that are available from the chemist or supermarket. These will really help.

With the divorce rates rising, inevitably there are far more single men and women of retirement age who want a friendship and sexual relationship without having to make a total commitment to a marriage again. This may mean over the years having one or more new partners with long sexual histories behind them.

With pregnancy a thing of the past, condoms might be the last thing on your mind, but whatever your age you could pick up a sexually transmitted disease including HIV/AIDS. So don't take risks, even if you have really fallen for someone. Use condoms to give yourself peace of mind, until you are absolutely sure of your partner's history and it seems safe to do otherwise.

Having a healthy sex life doesn't just mean having a good sex life. Staying healthy whilst enjoying sex has become more important than ever because diseases which are caught through sex have become more common. A new relationship or a number of partners can put your health at risk, so it is important to know the risks and not be complacent.

It is a sad day when you find you have been deceived and your partner is having an affair. All kinds of emotions tumble through your mind. Shall I go, shall I throw him or her out, how could they do this to me are just a few. Out of this comes anger, resentment and jealousy, and it is hard to know which way to turn.

Affairs happen when a relationship is not giving one partner what they need – maybe they are expecting too much, maybe their emotional needs are not being met. People often say that they still love their wife or husband and that their affair is something separate from this. The truth is, it isn't – one affects the other. Even if you find your partner has had an affair it can be possible to put your relationship back together again, so long as you see it as a joint problem that has to be solved together. Of course you will want to apportion blame and you wouldn't be normal if you didn't, but stop and look at all those years that have gone before – 30, 40 or even more. Are you willing to let go of these for someone who has only shared a tiny fraction of his or her time? I hope not. You will have much to build on, lots of memories, happy and sad, providing you are totally honest with each other from now on. You will be able to find the way forward again, but changes will have to be made along the way. This has been the crux of the whole of this chapter: change in attitudes, change in thoughts, change in ways, to become closer both romantically and sexually.

Finally, I would like to look at being experimental in your lovemaking, whether it is watching sexy videos together, using sex aids such as vibrators, or trying out different ways of making love. It is never too late to try something new so long as it is done with love and caring.

Postbag

Q.1 I know the caring way you deal with letters regarding sexual problems in latter years. I like your approach which is never dismissive. You understand that sex doesn't stop as you get older but for some of us who are becoming, or who are already, disabled this valuable part of a relationship is often lost. I found out my wife had had an affair because my disability made it difficult for me to make love. We are still together, I have angry feelings but understand as well. After all, I still have sexual feelings, but pain and discomfort seem to override these. Can you suggest any help for myself and others who face this problem?

You are right, people in their sixties, seventies and eighties find sex is a very important part of their relationship. I would like to put you in touch with an organization called SPOD (The Association to Aid the Sexual and Personal Relationships of People With a Disability). This was founded by carers concerned that the disabled person's sexual needs were being overlooked. Anyone contacting them, either by writing to SPOD, 286 Camden Road, London, N7 0BJ, or phoning 0171 607 8851, can get advice and details of regional and local contacts plus workshops and membership details. I hope you will be amongst the first to get advice that will help you put the sexual magic back into your relationship.

Q.2 I am writing on behalf of my husband because he is too embarrassed to seek help from our doctor or speak to anyone about his problem. For nearly a year he has been unable to have sex because of impotence. He gets sexual feelings for me but is not able to have intercourse. It has reached a stage where he won't even cuddle me, he turns over and goes to sleep. When I got him to talk about it he said he feels a failure and that he is letting me down. I think the problem is he drinks too much; he says this is rubbish. He has a few beers most evenings. He says if anything alcohol will make him uninhibited and able to have sex and not the reverse. What do you think?

There is a quotation from Macbeth which says 'Alcohol provoketh the desire but taketh away the performance', and I think this is often true. There are many causes of impotency, including tiredness, stress, certain medical conditions such as diabetes and some medications including those prescribed for high blood pressure. Emotional problems can also cause this, so encourage him to see his doctor.

Q.3 I am 61 and going out with a woman for the first time since I was widowed ten years ago. I want to be sexually involved with her but I am too embarrassed to do so. You see, I am not very well endowed in my private parts. My wife used to joke about it. What if this woman found me to be an inadequate lover? She is a very sensitive and caring woman but one never knows if she might react in the same way as my wife did.

Listen, if size had any bearing on the ability to be a good lover there would be a lot of disappointed men and women around. Lots of men worry about this, but there really is no need. It is unkind to tease someone about this kind of thing and I am sure it won't be a problem with this woman.

Q.4 Although I am 74 I still feel the urge to make love, but my wife, who is 13 years younger than me, takes a very discouraging attitude to sex. She says men keep their urges longer than women and it is quite natural to feel the way she does, fed up with it at her age. Is this true?

No, it isn't. These are your wife's feelings but they don't apply to every woman of her age. Many women come into their sexual peak in their forties, fifties or even later, often because there is no longer any fear of pregnancy. It really is a case of 'if you don't use it . . . you might lose it' when it comes to sexual desire. Many men and women enjoy sex into their eighties and say it has improved like wine as the years passed. Maybe your wife should look at her own sexuality, why she feels the way she does and if she wants to do anything about it. Don't apologize for feeling sexy, talk about this problem and try to reach some compromise.

Q.5 After I went through the menopause I found it difficult to make love with my husband because it was very uncomfortable. Because of this, our relationship suffered and sex became non-existent. Two years ago we divorced, which was very traumatic as we were both in our early sixties. We continued to see each other occasionally and the affection we used to have for each other returned, so much so we have moved back together, not married but thinking of it. However, the original problem is still with us. This time, though, we have talked about it, although I am embarrassed to see my doctor.

First let me congratulate you on getting back together. This really is lovely. What you describe sounds like vaginal dryness which is very common after the menopause, more than at other times in a woman's life. Unfortunately, when it occurs many women give up on their lovemaking. If you feel pain when you attempt to have intercourse you should see your doctor for advice. If you feel discomfort due to dryness then a simple remedy is to use a lubricant which you can obtain at the chemist.

People write to me and ask 'What is good sex?' The answer is 'Whatever pleases you as a couple and doesn't offend or affect anyone else'. I hope you find the closeness both romantically and sexually that you need, but whatever you want for your relationship be kind to each other and remember to say 'I love you' each day.

10

The sad times

Life can be pretty cruel at times. Just when you think you have got it on to an even keel something happens and what was a smooth path suddenly becomes a very rocky one. Although tragedy can strike at any time often it is in the latter years that it happens more frequently. Friends and loved ones die and loneliness takes the place of the closeness you once knew. In this chapter we will look at the emotions surrounding divorce, bereavement, loneliness, rejection, illness and what to do if you find out your partner is having an affair.

When parents die

Let us start with the very complex subject of bereavement. I describe it in this way because every bereavement is different, and how it affects people varies. To illustrate this I will tell you about several case histories, all different and each tugging at emotions.

Stan was 62 when his mother died. He was single and had always lived with her except for the two years when he did his national service. His father died when he was 15 and he had taken on the role of looking after his mother. Although he would have liked to have married and have a family it hadn't been the end of the world when it didn't happen. He'd had several girlfriends in his twenties and thirties and one serious relationship for five years in his forties. Unfortunately, this ended when they decided to get married and his mother wanted to live with them. The woman didn't like his mother, put her foot down and Stan was persuaded by his mother that she wasn't the one for him. The relationship foundered and Stan never met anyone else after this.

He settled into a quiet existence, taking outings and holidays with his mother and spending most of their time together. When the police arrived at his office to tell him that his mother, now 81, had died of a heart attack that morning in the shopping precinct, all Stan could think of was the ambulance he had seen with its blue light flashing as he drove back from a meeting. His mother must have been in this, and he had driven by not knowing what had happened.

Stan's grief was one of a child who had lost his mother. He missed her company and all the things that she did for him. He also felt at a loss when it came to making decisions. His mother had been a very dominant woman who expected to be consulted before he took any decisions. If he went against her wishes, she would punish him in some way or another. When she died there was not the relief that independence might have brought him, instead there was uncertainty, disorientation and anger that she had left him unprepared for a life on his own.

Stan never got over his mother's death, but coped by turning inwards on himself and becoming both the mother and the son. He would sit for hours turning over in his mind what his mother would want him to do about a certain situation. He found the house too large to cope with, put it on the market on the spur of the moment and then spent two whole agonizing days crying, telling himself that his mother was cross and then promising her he would keep the house. He then punished himself by cancelling the holiday he had booked. When I counselled Stan it was like talking to two people, with his mother's side being strongest, but gradually he came to terms with his grief and started to talk about his mother in past terms rather than in present ones.

When a son or daughter dies

Most parents imagine their children will outlive them and when they lose a son or a daughter it is a terrible shock that many never completely recover from. They learn to cope but that is an entirely different matter.

Madge, 38, had gone into hospital for a small operation and expected to be out the same evening. She left her children with her parents, Bill and Joan, in the morning, and with a cheery 'see you tonight' she and her husband drove off to the hospital. That was the last time they ever saw their daughter. She didn't come out of the anaesthetic and died on the operating table. Joan described their loss as one of having an arm amputated. It still feels as if it is there but it has gone. No one could have foreseen this tragedy, but Joan and Bill felt they had let Madge down in some way.

As an only child they had always lavished lots of love, care and attention on her and worried about her for the slightest cause. When Madge died they felt helpless. Up until then their energies had been channelled in her direction, now they had to find a new focus and a way of showing Madge their love for her went on. Madge's husband Geoff needed their help and support with the children otherwise he would have been unable to work. Sometimes he had to check the amount of spoiling that went on, but for the most part their shared grief brought them all very close and it was a great tribute to their daughter's memory. The youngest child, Amy, age five, summed it up when she said to her grandma 'I always say God bless Mummy and Daddy first when I say my prayers Grandma, then I ask both God and Mummy to look after you and Grandpa'.

Bill and Joan don't understand why their child was taken away from them. They are still angry, but the sheer need to be able to get on and look after the children gave them the emotional channel and prop that they needed to be able to cope with their grief.

When a partner dies

Both Phil and Sadie were widowed on the same day but the emotions each had were entirely different.

Phil's wife Eileen had died after a long illness with cancer. When Eileen's cancer was first diagnosed they had been devastated, they talked, wept and were angry together. Over the next two years they both came to terms with the fact that Eileen might not live for very long. They packed their days with things they had always wanted to do whilst Eileen was well enough to do them. When she became too ill to go out, they reminisced long into the night about their marriage and the happy times they had spent. Towards the end they talked about Eileen's funeral, how Phil would cope when she was no longer there and how they would meet up again when Phil's turn came. She told him he must take his chance to marry again if he met someone else and not feel guilty.

When Eileen died, Phil was glad she was no longer suffering, he missed her and yet he felt very peaceful inside. Over the two years, they had grieved together and now, although there was a sadness that Eileen was no longer there in body, Phil felt she visited him each day as she promised she would do until he could cope alone. Three years later Phil married his wife's cousin who was also a widow. Some might say that Phil was submerging his emotions after his wife died, but sometimes it is possible to share grief before a partner dies.

In many terminal cases such as this the couple never talk about what is going to happen and then when the inevitable happens so much has been left unsaid that the grief is much harder to bear. There are no set rules, each couple has to do what is best for them and what they can cope with.

Not everyone can cope with talking about dying. As a nation we are pretty bad about doing this. How many times have you heard people say 'if I should die, God forbid'? The first move towards talking as this couple did can come from either partner, but how it progresses on from there will depend on how the one who is suffering from the illness copes with it.

When Sadie's husband had a heart attack and died they were going through a very ferocious and violent patch in their marriage. In fact, they were about to divorce and had even been arguing that day.

You can be forgiven for thinking that Sadie might have thought she had been given a happy release from this marriage, but in fact she went to pieces. She suffered a very long and guilt-ridden bereavement, constantly blaming herself for her husband's death, asking herself if his behaviour was because he had felt ill for a long time, whether she should have been more tolerant. She regretted the harsh words of the past between them.

This is a very common occurrence in bad relationships. I received a letter from a woman in her eighties who had wished her husband dead on many occasions before he died. Since then she had spent ten years blaming herself for his death, believing she had killed him through her wicked thoughts.

In situations like this it is very important to realize that guilt is one of many emotions that come after any death. Whether it is wishing you had called the doctor sooner, recognized the symptoms, not been dismissive when he or she said they felt unwell . . . most people who are bereaved feel this at some stage or another. You can't live with someone for 30 years or more without experiencing grief when they die, whatever your relationship was like. Shock, anxiety, guilt, disbelief it has happened and even anger with the deceased because they have died is all part of the grieving pattern. Not everyone experiences all these emotions and not everyone experiences them in the same order or grieves for the same length of time. Some may grieve for a few weeks or months, others for several years, neither is right or wrong.

Bereavement

Friends and relatives often say 'You will feel better after the funeral'. The truth is you won't. In fact, those first few days leading up to the funeral are usually so busy that the widow or widower doesn't have time to sit and think. Often they are surrounded by family and friends, and it is not until everyone disappears after the funeral that they are alone with their thoughts. Friends and relations often try to hurry people through their grief, but I believe this is wrong. They will try to get the bereaved person to 'get out', to 'get on with their lives', but who are they doing this for? Is it for the bereaved or for themselves because they find anything to do with death hard to cope with?

Many people worry because they think they can hear their loved ones' voices after they have died. I think you have to liken this to when your children were babies and they cried constantly, then they stopped but you could still hear the crying. It is almost as if, like a recording machine, we record the voices within us. If you experience this, don't worry; it is very common and many people find it comforting.

Probably the most hurtful thing for anyone who has been bereaved is when people pass by on the other side of the road, pretending they haven't seen the person because they don't know what to say. It is bad enough being bereaved without being made to feel a social outcast as well. I firmly believe that when you live with someone that you love, be it your partner, sister, brother, parent, child or friend, you invest a part of yourself in them and when they die a part of you goes with them. You won't ever get this part back, but gradually you will replace it with other things as you move through the grieving period. This must be at your own pace, don't be hurried by anyone. Go with the flow and you will eventually find peace of mind.

Rejection

Rejection is something most of us fear, whether it is within our personal or business life. Applying for a job, whether it is paid or voluntary work, takes courage, but this can be severely dented if you are rejected as being too old once you have retired or not quite what the employer or organization is looking for. It takes even more courage to re-embark on a new relationship and to ask someone out that you have had your eye on for some time. If they refuse, the pain of rejection is acute. You may smile and say it doesn't matter, but, boy, does it hurt! Whether you are 16 or 60 it can feel the same.

All of us put ourselves up hundreds of times during our lifetimes to the risk of being rejected. We offer help, time, skills, love, caring, even our hearts and sometimes they are refused. How you deal with it depends on how much you value yourself. If you allow yourself to feel rejected, you are allowing others to undervalue you. Instead, take the 'I tried it and it wasn't what they needed' attitude. This shifts the rejection and the balance squarely on to the other person. If they can't see your value, then that's their problem!

Loneliness

After bereavement, loneliness brings in the highest number of letters from senior citizens who are unhappy. There are varying degrees of loneliness and many causes, but most loneliness will cause misery. Some men and women class loneliness as not having a partner of the opposite sex, whilst others have no friends at all. As people get older, their friends and family die and it is not easy to replace them, but it can be done if you are prepared to work at it and put yourself out. Sitting at home feeling sorry for yourself when you have your health and all your faculties won't get you anywhere. Rushing out of the door searching for friends isn't going to work either. What you have to do is plan.

Make a list of the things you enjoy doing that will bring you in contact with other people. Going for long walks alone or sticking your head under the bonnet of a car won't work, but if you join a walking club, a car maintenance or veteran car club then it will bring you in contact with like-minded people who may also be looking for a friend.

'I don't like to push myself forward' or 'I keep myself to myself' are comments often heard, sayings that are 100 per cent guaranteed to keep you lonely. If you won't push yourself forward, who will? Keep yourself to yourself and it's a promise of total privacy for as long as you want it. Lonely people are often shy, and that is understandable, but some people are lazy and expect others to come running to them offering friendship. Once you have worked out what you enjoy socially and where you can meet other people, then you have to be prepared to take the bull by the horns and go for it. I have spoken to many people in the course of my research for this book and shy and lonely people say it is getting over that first hurdle that is hardest, the rest falls into place and gets easier.

Feeling disloyal often leads to widows and widowers being lonely.

Beryl was one who fell into this category. After 40 years of marriage she felt total loyalty to her late husband and felt her place was in the home he had built and furnished for her. She would allow herself to go shopping, but the rest of the time she spent indoors cleaning and polishing the shrine to her late husband. She seldom saw anyone and when neighbours called by she never asked them in and actively discouraged any further calls. She was healthy and active and yet she made herself housebound and very lonely.

Yet there are disabled people who get out against quite hard odds and manage to enjoy life to the full. They know the way to deal with obstacles in life and we can learn an awful lot from them. There are lots of shy and lonely people of all ages out there, but you have to make some effort to start the friendship ball rolling.

Illness

When illness strikes, often the carers suffer just as much as the patient. If one partner has a terminal illness it can be physically and mentally tiring for the carer, as well as emotionally scarring. There will be times when you will think that you can't cope, you would like to walk away, or you wish you could wake up and find it was all a bad dream. All these emotions are perfectly normal, as is the anger you feel that this is happening to the partner you love. Most people will suddenly realize that there are things they wish they had done either with or for their partner. Remember, it may not be too late to put this right.

Being a carer doesn't make you a superman or superwoman, so accept your limitations and any help offered. Of course you would like to sit with your partner all night, but you need to get rest so that you can cope during the day. Don't be afraid to take rests when you can and accept that someone else may have to take a turn at being with your partner whilst you sleep. Several hours' sleep could mean the difference between giving your time gladly or ending up resentful.

It is natural to want to keep your partner at home for as long as possible to give them the best care you can, but sometimes a short stay or being in hospital for a longer term can give them the best care they can have. You can only do your best.

Regrets

Along with retirement often come regrets. Maybe you wish you had been more ambitious at work, been more self-assertive or followed your heart's desire. If you are single, separated or divorced, you may wish things were different. Perhaps you gave up on the chance to marry to care for your mum or dad. At the time, this may have seemed the right thing to do but now you regret having given up on the love and companionship and wish you had someone to share your life with.

A divorce that may have taken place some years ago can still have long-lasting effects into retirement, especially if you are still alone and you see your ex-partner happily married and financially secure. You can't turn back the clock, but you should try to get things into perspective. It's all too easy to look back with a rosy glow, remembering the good things and regretting past decisions. So try to remember the reasons why you separated or got divorced in the first place and accept that these were right for you then and are right for you now. Although regrets can help us to focus on the negative things we have done in our lives, it is important to remember that they can also be a stumbling-block to moving forward in our lives.

Postbag

Q.1 My husband has Alzheimer's disease and gets very angry and abusive, so much so that I spoke to my GP and said I couldn't cope. He arranged for my husband to go to a day centre three times a week. I know I should be grateful and put this time to good use, but he makes me feel so guilty for sending him there that I don't.

There is no need to feel guilty, you need a break from the caring. Your husband's behaviour is erratic whether he goes to the centre or not. If he was at home I dare say he would behave in such a way that you would feel guilty about something else. The best use you can make of these days is to put your feet up and have a good rest.

Q.2 People don't understand what it is like to be lonely. I live alone since my brother died, I have never married or had friends. My brother and I were great friends and there didn't seem to be the need for outsiders. Now he has gone, the days are very long and empty, no one seems to want to know.

Having been a loner for so long it would be hard for others to realize that you are now looking for friends. You have to change the vibes that you give out so that they can see your offer of friendship. There are so many lonely people about that you could befriend. Start by becoming a member of the League of Friends at your local hospital. Helping in the cafeteria or visiting patients on the ward with the library trolley will give you the chance to meet people and become more at ease.

Q.3 My husband and I divorced because our children encouraged it. They said they loved us but it hurt them to see us tearing each other apart. Now we are both lonely and neither of us is happy. We would like to give it another try but we know the children will throw their hands up in horror.

Well let them! Sounds to me that you have let your children have too much control of your lives. Now is the time to make your own decisions. But don't drift back together for the wrong reasons, it has to be because you genuinely want to be together.

Q.4 I have worked for and been in love with my boss for 13 years. We are both in our late fifties, we get on well and when he divorced two years ago we talked for hours and became close.

On several occasions we went to the theatre or for dinner, but then these outings stopped because people in the office found out. Despite this, I always hoped we would get together again and that by the time I retired we would be a couple. We often laughed and said we were saving ourselves for each other in our old age. I have never been married, by the way.

Three weeks ago he went skiing and came back and told me he had met someone else. He is talking commitment to her and I am devastated and feel totally rejected. When he told me I cried and poured out my feelings. He was embarrassed and said he had never had those kind of feelings towards me. He has been very kind but I can feel the tension between us. Today he asked if I would like to be transferred to another branch to make a new start – at my age! The job on offer is working with one of the directors, with more money, but I don't know what to do. The thought of not seeing him is worse than being rejected, and I feel such a fool.

I felt very sorry for you when I read your letter. Sadly, a relationship between a secretary and her boss seldom turns into any long-term relationship. As for feeling a fool, don't be so hard on yourself, maybe you did read more into the relationship than there was, but maybe he enjoyed your ardent attention and encouraged it. Theatre trips and dining out are not the kind of thing you offer if there are not some feelings there. My guess is he liked your company a lot but suddenly love hit him firmly between the eyes and he was too wrapped up in his own feelings to stop and think of yours. If the opportunity to transfer to another branch, with the offer of a better job, is available, I would take it. Yes, you will miss him, but you need a fresh start if you are ever going to be able to get on with your life.

The sad times will come, but it depends on how you meet them as to how you will cope. Remember three things:

- Don't expect too much of yourself.
- Don't expect to cope overnight.
- Don't fight emotions that are perfectly normal, as they are all a very necessary part of the healing process to get your life back together again.

11

Life is for living

Ask anyone who has been retired for some years and they will tell you they don't know where all the hours in the day disappear to. But at the onset it can bring a mixture of anticipation, excitement and apprehension. After all, 2,000 extra hours to fill each year does seem an awful lot.

Have fun

You will find ways of filling these hours, but before you do, think carefully, put a value on these hours, just as you would your money. To live a full life in retirement is one thing, to live a rich and happy one is an entirely different matter. As we discussed in another chapter, there will be practical things that you will want to do, such as gardening, decorating and even a part-time job, but what about the fun side, how much of this have you been having lately? If the answer is very little, then now is the time to put this right. Not everyone can afford to rush off to Disneyland, but something that was said to me and my family by a man at the entrance to the Magic Kingdom a couple of years ago puts into words what I am trying to get over to you. As we approached the turnstiles, he looked at us, and with a wide grin asked, 'Have you come to have fun?' In unison, my husband, myself and my children, then 11 and 14, replied with a resounding 'Yes'. As we turned to go into the Magic Kingdom, I thought 'What must he have thought? . . . He was obviously talking to the children.' I then heard him say very much the same thing to the couple behind, who must have been in their eighties, but from the look of excitement on their faces they could have been eight as they also said 'Yes'.

A lot of people see age as a barrier to many of the good things in life. They become old before their time, and staid in their ways, they seldom smile or laugh and everything is an effort for them. It is never too late to change your attitude to life and the way you enjoy yourself. We all need to feel good about ourselves and what we do, otherwise we fall in to the 'gloom and doom' mode. Someone once said that every time you sigh you take a day off your life. I doubt if this can be proved, but I think there could be some basis for this statement because how we feel inside will affect our physical well-being.

Whether you can take a holiday or not will very much depend on your financial position. Those that can afford to travel abroad will know the excitement of reaching a new destination with a different culture. To be able to see the mountains, the oceans, the deserts and all the wonders of the world can't fail to give you a feeling of contentment and happiness. If it doesn't, then there must be other problems that you need to sort out at home and in your relationship.

For those who can't or don't want to travel abroad there is so much to see and do in this country and it need not cost you a lot, as you will see from Mollie and Jim and Kathy and Mike's stories. We'll start with Kathy's dreams to travel all around the coast of England when they retired.

Although Mike knew of Kathy's pipe dream, he never thought she would really want to do it, so it came as a bit of a surprise when he found her poring over advertisements in the newspapers looking for a dormobile. He still thought it was unlikely, even when she dragged him off to look at two. The first was very dilapidated but the second was in reasonable condition and the price wasn't bad for the year and mileage. Mike had to agree that it was very compact and he hoped he wouldn't have to spend one night in it, let alone weeks or months! Back home, Kathy didn't give up and the following day Mike, in a rather bemused state, found himself parting with £1,100 to make Kathy's dream come true.

They worked on the dormobile for two months, until Mike retired. Three days later they had a big sendoff party when family and friends brought gifts of tinned food, wine and other items to stock up the dormobile. It was bursting at the seams by the time they left. Soon Mike was in the spirit of the adventure. They had intended to be away from April to July, but enjoyed it so much that they didn't return until October.

Looking tanned, well and now the proud owners of two second-hand bikes they returned to their home. One of the problems they had encountered was that if they needed to go shopping they both had to leave the campsite together because they only had the dormobile to travel around in. On one occasion, in the height of the season when they were at Morecambe, they had come back to find someone else was on their spot. So the bikes meant they could go out independently or together and not have to worry. The last I heard was that they were planning to go to France. Who knows where they will go after this?

Mollie and Jim retired with nothing other than their state pension and for them holidays seemed impossible. Living in the suburbs, they would spend many days using their bus passes to visit London, but Mollie still wanted to go on holiday. One day her daughter showed her an advert from someone in Devon who wanted to do a house swap for a month so that they could have a base near London. Losing no time, Mollie phoned and six weeks later her daughter was waving goodbye to them as they left on the train. Since then they have had house swaps in seaside towns all along the south coast, in Bath and in Edinburgh. Their children buy their rail tickets as presents for birthdays and Christmas. As Jim puts it, 'It's a real home from home and so far we have never come back to any problems.'

Nancy lives opposite me, and at the age of 80 she absolutely oozes fun. It is hard to catch her in as she is always out enjoying herself. She plays bridge, enjoys crafts and is out most evenings doing sequence or country and western dancing at a nearby holiday camp. Her sense of humour and fun is so sharp that everyone, even youngsters, enjoys having her around. Nancy was widowed when she was 73 and although she still misses her husband Cliff it is a tribute to the good times they shared that she has carried on doing the things they enjoyed together.

It is so important to have a social life. This is something you have to carve out for yourself and whether it is through clubs, friends, sport or courses it pays to make the most of your leisure time. Remember, you can always try something and give it up if you don't like it and then move on to something else. The important factor is to enjoy it. This will give you a sense of lightness within yourself, which in turn makes life worth living. If you have a partner, then you will need to talk about your leisure time and how it is to be divided up. There will be things your partner wants to do that you won't want to do, and vice versa. There is nothing wrong with pursuing your own interests as well as things together.

Religion may seem far removed from fun, but is it? Find an inner peace with God and you may well be more open to the opportunities and good things around you. There are many paths to God and each of us finds own way. Some may want the regular visits to church, others may prefer to sit quietly alone and talk to God by themselves. Do whatever feels right for you. Those that belong to a church often find great satisfaction in the pastoral and social side of the church. Getting together for harvest suppers, fêtes, barn dances, discos and other events organized by the church can be very enjoyable.

If you are the kind of person who gets easily het up, it would pay to take up a hobby at home that helps you relax. The list is endless, but here are just a few to be going on with:

embroidery, tatting, crochet, model-making, oil painting, sculpture, candle-making, water-colours, collage, soft furnishings, wireless ham, flower-arranging, etching, writing poetry or a book, fly-tying, pewter and copper work.

Friendship

Friends are very important in retirement, to share both time and confidences with. Don't limit yourself just to friends of the same age-group as you are. You will keep a much broader outlook on life if you have friends of all ages. Although it may seem harder to make new friends as you get older, it isn't if you set your mind to it. Don't wait for people to befriend you, keep a warm open attitude to the people you meet and you will become very popular.

The way you look, stand, smile and dress influences the way people are attracted to you. Don't wear drab clothes in black, grey and brown all the time. Even if you can't afford new things, the charity shops now offer good quality clothes at reasonable prices. Make sure you have something in your wardrobe in warm colours such as red, wine, burgundy, rust or orange. These are all positive colours and you will be surprised how much better you will be if on days when you feel depressed or miserable you wear these colours. Lilac, mauve, lavender and all kinds of blue (not turquoise) are all good colours to wear if you are feeling unwell. Green and turquoise will be restful, and on days when you need a bit of sunshine or sparkle in your life wear yellow, gold or silver.

The colours you wear also affect the people you meet. I visited a friend who was very ill and wore a warm orange dress with a long rust coat over it. My friend was too restless to talk to me at the time, but later she told her husband that the colour of what I was wearing made her feel calm and more positive.

If you are married or living with someone, you will probably have joint friends as well as ones of your own. Retirement is no reason to give up on personal friends, in fact it is even more reason to hang on to them. Being together 24 hours a day can put a strain on both of you. If you can spend time with a friend occasionally, then you will both be better for it. Some people would be horrified if anyone suggested to them that they went to the pub, but the fact is more and more people drink non-alcoholic drinks because they drive, and pubs are gearing themselves to serving good food and hot drinks as well as alcoholic ones. Your local could be the place to meet new people and gain friends. Many organize darts, snooker and pool competitions, as well as quiz and karaoke nights. The

British Legion and many other social and community clubs arrange a wide range of social events as well as having a bar. It may not sound as if it is for you, but walk past any pub, club or Legion and you will hear the laughter of people enjoying themselves. Can you say the same if anyone walked past your house?

Laughter is something that many relationships lack. It is as if the light has been switched off and no one can find the switch. Do you sit in silence watching the television every evening? Do you and your partner seldom speak? Ask yourself how long ago you laughed and when the last time was that you had any fun. Whatever your age, you deserve to enjoy yourself. Many people don't because they can't be bothered to make the effort, yet some take each day against all the odds and live it to the full.

Jamie is one of these. He lost his legs in the war and has been in a wheelchair ever since. He told me he could have sat there and done nothing. Instead, over the years, he has raced in his wheelchair, played sports, played darts for his local team, and navigates for a friend when they go out rallying. Jamie's wife has to be quick to catch him as he goes from one thing to another. He even goes swimming with his grandchildren, although he describes himself as a cork because he bobs around in the water! He is never too proud to ask for help, and I hope his story will help other retired disabled people.

Postbag

Q.1 Although retired, I still get invited out by my ex-colleagues from the bank where I used to work. This happens about twice a month. We have a real laugh and I enjoy these outings, but I am worried that they may invite me out of habit and because they wouldn't want to upset me by not doing so. You see, they are all in their forties and early fifties and I can't see why they would want to include me when I am so much older. I am 63. Should I decline next time they phone?
Whatever for? If they wanted to drop you, your retirement would have given them the opportunity – they have to make an effort to phone and invite you. Be honest with yourself, would they really do this if you were in the way? No!

Q.2 As a regular churchgoer my husband is very involved. He has been made a church warden since he retired, which has given him a real boost. I don't go to church, it is not for me, but John thinks I should make the effort for him and attend all the social events, as well as the services on Sunday. I would be a hypocrite if I did and have told him this. My belief is in goodness and in peace and I meditate and send out good feelings to those I love. This is the first time we have ever had a problem between us like this. What should I do?

You could compromise and go and sit at the back of the church and be with your own thoughts rather than join in the service. This way John would be happy knowing you were there. John may worry that you are not sharing his faith, but he has to understand that you must find your own inner peace in your own way. He may also worry about what other people in the church may think, but you must not let this affect you or your decision. Go to the social events and support him in any way that you feel you can.

Q.3 I went to the seaside with the Darby and Joan club for the first time in 70 years and at the age of 79 I rolled up my skirt, stuffed it in my knickers and paddled in the sea. It was great, I was back in time on the Sunday-school outing. I stood by the sea and sang one of the songs from the past and I laughed until I nearly cried. Others from the club turned away and hardly anyone spoke to me on the coach going back. I was just enjoying myself, but later my neighbour told me I was an embarrassment.

How sad that these folk have forgotten what it is like to be childlike and free from inhibitions. I wish they had joined you in the sea and then they would have known the happiness that you felt. Don't let them ever put you off enjoying yourself, let them have their staid ways. You know there is something far better to be had – so, sing away.

Q.4 I have always found it hard to make friends and for the first time in over 60 years I have made friends, with a man who has moved into the house next door. We get on well and have very similar interests. My problem is my wife is jealous of the friend. She sulks if I stay talking to him for too long. When I said he had invited me to his indoor bowling club she got really angry and said that if I went she wouldn't be there when I came back. So the result was that I stayed in and we didn't talk for the rest of the evening. I have always been there for her and it is the first time I have ever wanted to do something for myself. Is it wrong to want this? I am 66.

Take a good look at your relationship. Have you and your wife always done everything together? Do you ever take her out? Has she got any friends? It sounds as if she is resentful and also worried that she is going to be left out. I think it would be sad to give up on this friendship and you should be free to go bowling with him if you choose. Your wife sounds as if she needs a bit of love and attention so that she doesn't feel threatened in this way. She also needs some hobbies and friends of her own. Try to be understanding. Basically, she is frightened that you won't have time for her.

I leave the final paragraph of this chapter to a quote from Jamie whose ability to cope with his disability is an inspiration to us all.

> People accept you as you are.
> If you don't make the most of your life
>   then you will only have yourself to blame.
> There are lots of good things out there if you go out
>   and look for them, they won't come looking for you.
> Life can be dull and boring if you let it,
>   but it can also be fun.

12

The best years are still to come

Dear Friend

We have travelled a long way since the first chapter of this book, touched on many memories and probably some raw nerves. All the way through I have put emphasis on honesty and the need to talk things through when you are unhappy. I hope you will see the benefits of this. Too many people keep all their disappointments, anger and hurt feelings inside themselves, they say nothing for the sake of peace and quiet because they are frightened, don't want to rock the boat, or because they accept this as their lot in life. What I hope you can see is that you don't have to put up with unhappiness. Of course there will be things such as bereavement, divorce, a home you don't like or lack of money which cannot be altered, but the way you feel inside about your purpose in life, your relationship and retirement can be changed.

Sometimes life may seem stormy, but think how beautiful a rainbow can be when the storm subsides. Some of the exercises I have asked you to undertake may have been painful but I hope you stick with them so that you take charge of your life rather than letting it take charge of you. If you are about to retire, I hope you will set off along that long sandy path with excitement in your heart. Don't let other peoples' dire tales put you off – you are unique. How you use these days, weeks and months ahead of you is up to you. It will be different, but that is good. Think of it as a long holiday, one where you can pick and choose what you want to do. No more having to rush in the mornings to get to work, no more snatched lunches, no more doing a repetitive job or one that you don't enjoy. You are the lucky one, because there are so many good things ahead.

Twenty or more years ago a book like this wouldn't have been written because retirement was looked upon as a time to rest after a long life's work. People were more inclined to put up with whatever came their way, there were fewer pension schemes around and people's attitude to retired people was almost one of dismissal. They had had their time, they didn't need much; basically, people were saying they were past it. Today the retired are looked upon as a valuable sector of the community. Thousands of voluntary agencies would have had to close if it wasn't for the generosity of time given by our senior citizens. In the paid sector, many companies employ valued workers who are over 60. Retired people are active in local government, on school governing boards and in many sectors of the community. Thank goodness the 'old-age pensioner' title has given way to the 'senior citizen' one, a title I feel gives a dignity to the retiring person. At the same time, the word 'citizen' confirms that he or she is very much part of the community. Far better than being labelled 'old' and feeling you are on the scrap heap.

There is so much out there to be part of, whether you are retired already or just about to retire. Many people will tell you that they have found more happiness since they retired than ever before. What they may not realize is that they have found the secret of happiness. Things around you will affect the way you feel, but they won't give you the answer to happiness. You have to come to know that happiness comes from within yourself. If you can clear your mind of all the things that bother you, think positively and count your blessings, you will find this happiness and feel at one with yourself. Once you find this, your inner joy will shine through to those around you. People will want your company, you will be loved and respected. Things in your life will suddenly slot into place. You won't be one of those who sit around moaning there is nothing to do after 60 and that the world is against you. Instead, you will feel emotionally secure and be free to enjoy the best years of your life!

Find your rainbow and be happy

Love

Vicky